BREATHE EASY WITH RETIRE FOR L.I.F.E.™

A FOUR-STEP PLAN TO UNCOMPLICATE YOUR RETIREMENT

MATTHEW SCHULLER

AMY BUTTELL

I dedicate this book to my two sons, Hudson and Beckett; to my amazing wife, Ali, who has always supported me and been by my side; and to my parents, Larry and Bonnie. Lastly, I dedicate this book to my Lord and Savior who gave me the abilities to do what I love.

DISCLOSURE

may introduce insurance products, such as an annuity, as a potential solution. Social Security benefit payout rates can and will change at the sole discretion of the Social Security Administration. For more information, please direct your clients to a local Social Security Administration office or visit www.ssa.gov.

No Investment strategy can guarantee a profit or protect against loss in a period of declining values. Any references to protection benefits or lifetime income generally refer to fixed insurance products, never securities or investment products. Insurance and annuity products are backed by the financial strength and claims-paying ability of the issuing insurance company. Annuities are insurance products backed by the claims-paying ability of the issuing company; they are not FDIC insured; are not obligations or deposits of, and are not guaranteed or underwritten by any bank, savings and loan or credit union or its affiliates; are unrelated to and not a condition of the provision or term of any banking service or activity. Annuities are long-term products of the insurance industry designed for retirement income. They contain some limitations, including possible withdrawal charges and a market value adjustment that could affect contract values. Product features vary by state and restrictions may apply, including possible withdrawal charges. Please contact your agent or the Company for more information. Guaranteed lifetime income available through annuitization or the purchase of an optional lifetime income rider, a benefit for which an annual premium is charged. All examples provided are hypothetical and provided for illustrative purposes only; it does not represent a real-life scenario and should not be construed as advice designed to meet the particular needs of an individual's situation.

CONTENTS

CHAPTER 1

THE RETIRE FOR L.I.F.E.™ PROGRAM

AS A DISCIPLINE, financial planning came into existence a little more than 50 years ago.[1] Within the realm of financial planning, retirement planning and retirement income planning are much more recent developments. With 10,000 baby boomers retiring every day, the limits of conventional retirement planning are being tested and redefined.[2]

Because retirement planning is such a young discipline, practitioners don't have more experienced colleagues or decades-old bodies of research to rely upon for guidance. That's created somewhat of a Wild West approach in which financial advisors attempt to guide pre-retirees and retirees as best they can.

While I have no doubt that most financial advisors are well-intentioned, many may lack the knowledge and experience to properly help their clients prepare for and live through increasingly longer retirements. For the sake of their clients, financial advisors need to develop more systematic processes that focus on a client's objectives and a product-agnostic retirement income planning process.

After years spent as a financial wholesaler, I became a financial advisor focused on retirement income planning. That experience as a financial wholesaler gave me a window into contemporary retirement planning practices because I visited thousands of financial advisors across the country. My job involved traveling all over America, helping financial advisors incorporate retirement income planning products to improve and grow their practices.

This decade-long experience was educational and inspired me to become a retirement income advisor. In my travels meeting thousands of advisors, I came to realize that many financial advisors are far too focused on products. This means that advisors tend to build retirement plans around specific products, rather than utilizing a specific process designed to mitigate a client's retirement income risks.

Many advisors I met with were obsessively attached to a specific product or specific set of products. I can't tell you how often I met with advisors who would only sell investment products such as stocks, bonds, exchange-traded funds or mutual funds, refusing to consider insurance products like annuities. At the same time, I met equally as many advisors who were insurance-only agents, refusing to get the appropriate license and use investment products. In other words, these advisors let products–rather than client objectives and needs–drive the retirement income planning process.

Meeting these advisors led me to wonder how they came to believe in such different approaches while performing many of the same services for their clients. I developed close relationships with them through training and practice-building activities. These advisors were not fly-by-night. Many were at the top of their field and brought a deep attitude of care and concern for their clients. What I came to realize is that these advisors–and the industry–confuses the financial plan and its goals with the specific tools available for achieving it. In other words, if the only tool you have is a hammer, everything you see is a nail. If, as an advisor, you only know insurance products like annuities, then annuities will seem like the only logical solution for retirement planning problems. On the other hand, if all you know are investments, then investments are the only solution for creating a retirement income plan.

Let me use a metaphor. My father was an entrepreneur in construction. I worked for him as a kid. When building a house, for example, guys like my dad will use any number of tools: hammers, buzzsaws, nail guns, whatever gets the job done. In construction, there's no such thing as a bad tool, just tools that work well or less well for certain tasks. While you can technically use a hammer to hang siding, if I tried to do that instead of using a nail gun, my dad would look at me like I was crazy.

Working in financial services I came to realize that, just like in construction, there are no such things as bad tools—just financial products that work differently to accomplish the job. And unfortunately, I also realized that a lot of the advisors I worked with were in a similar position as the kid who uses a hammer to hang siding. They were focused on using an individual product, like a 401(k), or an annuity for that matter, to build the whole house, so to speak. Or when they found that didn't work, they still ended up using the tool they knew the best and subbing in others that were not well adapted to the task at hand.

In my experience, only in rare cases were these advisors starting with a plan and a well-defined financial planning process and *then* deciding which tool was the best for specific parts of the job. Back to the construction analogy—imagine trying to build a house without a design. Instead of using an architectural plan that shows exactly where every element of the home goes, a builder would instead mash together whatever materials were available haphazardly. What kind of structure would result from that approach? Not one that you would want to live in, more than likely. Retirement income planning is the same. Without a plan and a process, there is no way to know whether the right result can be or will be achieved.

The philosophy I try to bring to advising clients approaching retirement is product agnostic. I tell them that *there's really no bad tool, just bad tools when it comes to this or that specific job.* My process is to use tools to create strategies that include both guaranteed income products such as annuities or bonds, and products designed for growth potential such as stocks or mutual funds. I also use a collaborative planning process with detailed input from the client.

I think of the process like organizing the junk drawer. In your kitchen or somewhere in your house, you likely have a junk drawer where all the spare tools you might need to fix something are located. When most clients come to me, they have what we could describe as a retirement investing junk drawer. They might have a 401(k) from this job, or a pension or IRA from another one, bonds they got from an inheritance, and other things. They've accumulated these different financial tools throughout their working life. What they don't know, and what I help them to do, is to figure out which of the tools they have accumulated are right for the different tasks involved in fixing up their retirement future house. I help them dump out the junk drawer and organize the tools.

Retire for L.I.F.E.™ is a retirement planning process that fits the tools–the financial products–to the tasks involved in the overall plan for retirement. In the rest of the chapter, I summarize the basics of my planning philosophy and give an outline of what you can expect to learn as you read the rest of the book.

PLANNING PHILOSOPHY: THINKING OUTSIDE THE BOX

I always tell potential clients who come to my seminars that they will learn to think "outside the box" when it comes to retirement planning. It's kind of an overused cliché, but I mean it in a very specific way. Often, they have developed thought patterns about finances based on experiences they have had in their working lives. Essentially, they've developed a "box" around their thinking about finance. However, retirement requires very different thinking because the goals of retirement are different than saving for retirement. That's why I suggest out of the box thinking—because it's easy to make mistakes based on old thought patterns.

Retire for L.I.F.E.™ aims to help clients break out of the boxes that constrain their thinking and conceptions around retirement and distributing retirement savings during that period. Many investors do not understand the difference between what financial advisors call the accumulation and distribution phases of retirement. Briefly, in the accumulation phase, you are saving for retirement. That phase usually lasts many years during your entire working life, as you save money that may be matched by your employer and then invest it so that it will grow into enough savings to support you in retirement. Because saving for retirement lasts decades, you benefit from a long time horizon for investing. That means you have plenty of time to ride out the ebb and flow of the stock market.

Whether you're an advisor or a retirement investor, you probably remember how badly the market declined during the 2007-2009 financial crisis–in fact, from the peak of the market right before the crisis to the bottom of the market during that crisis, the S&P 500 index fell by 57.7 percent.[3] While nearly every investor who participated in the market during that time was spooked by that decline, younger investors, many years away from retirement, could afford to ride out that decline. In fact, by staying in the market and buying more shares of stock through mutual funds in their 401(k) plans, these investors dollar-cost-averaged down so that when the market bounced back, the value of their portfolios increased. However, for investors who were near retirement, or who had just retired, that decline was a disaster, and some were not able to recover.

Timing is critical. When you have the luxury of time, as investors do who are in the early or middle part of the accumulation phase of retirement, you can relax during market downturns, understanding that you don't need those assets to pay your bills and that the market will bounce back. However, when you are just about to retire, have just retired, or are in retirement, severe market declines can spell disaster. This is exactly why you need to approach investing in retirement and right before retirement differently than investing during the accumulation phase.

A long-term perspective is another important component of a healthy approach to retirement investing. It's useful to know that since the market emerged from the Great Recession at the end of 2009, the S&P 500 has returned 14.2% on an average annual return basis through the end of 2021.[4] Over time, the market's bias is generally upward with bear markets occurring around 3.5 years apart from each other while economic recessions happen on average every four years.[56]

In addition to timing and long-term perspective, there is the additional layer of personality when it comes to investing. Personality traits can also mislead you when it comes to investing. One of the boxes that every investor needs to break out of is their approach to retirement. By nature and conditioning, you're likely to be either a conservative or an aggressive investor. But someone who has aggressively and successfully invested for years while they're working might find that in retirement, that same strategy which made them successful earlier puts their guaranteed income at risk in retirement. When planning for retirement, it's a good idea to open up your mind to different ideas and forget about your preconceived notions of retirement. When you open your mind, it's easier to understand how to pick the right tool for the job rather than just doing what you've always done.

Besides behavioral bias, another box that you need to break out of when thinking about retirement is confirmation bias. Confirmation bias is everywhere, not just in investing. It's the tendency to seek out information which supports our previously held beliefs. Someone who is convinced of a liberal or conservative viewpoint, when looking at the news for example, is going to gravitate to channels, websites, authors and anchors who will tell them news that confirms those viewpoints or interpret the news in a way that underlines what they already believe. That means you learn over time to filter out sources and stories that conflict with your beliefs.

Specifically, confirmation bias in investing means that investors over-emphasize information that goes along with what they already believe while discounting information that conflicts with these perceptions. For example, a client who holds a lot of investments in tech might, when watching CNBC, only absorb the good news about tech while ignoring the bad, or tune out stories that bode ill about the specific companies they invest in.

In fact, some financial advisors believe that confirmation bias interferes with sound decision making because it leads investors to become overly concentrated in a particular stock or sector. Over concentration can create problems in a retirement portfolio because the portfolio can become over-concentrated in certain risky sectors, creating the potential for a large decline during a recession or bear market. Also, such concentration creates vulnerability to company and sector-specific downturns, causing portfolios to get misaligned with long-term goals and risk profiles. Finally, confirmation bias short-circuits the process of taking a realistic view of market conditions. Clients will focus on some expert opinions and ignore others, leading to decisions based on incomplete information, which can go very wrong down the road.[7]

Confirmation bias affects advisors as well as clients. In fact, what I have encountered in my career as a wholesaler and what I have described above is a massive case of collective confirmation bias. There are too many advisors seeking information that confirms their belief that a certain mutual fund, or annuity, is the right product. Then, based on that belief, they build a plan around that tool only. Unfortunately, that tool is not a retirement plan designed to meet specific objectives. Instead, it is a product that they have been trained or conditioned to believe in through their experience and perceptions. My philosophy of solving retirement issues and tailoring the product tools to match needs aims to break the cycle of confirmation bias for the advisor as well as the client.

BOOK OVERVIEW

This book is designed to help you, the consumer, use a retirement income planning process with products or tools that are right for your particular situation. Following this program will help you position your retirement in the most efficient and effective way. By reading this book, you will learn the specific processes involved in creating a retirement plan.

In the next two chapters, I outline the well-known and newer risks involved in retirement. The traditional risks that retirement planners tend to look at are longevity, healthcare and long-term care expenses, inflation and market volatility, which I address in Chapter 2. In Chapter 3, I draw attention to the sequence of returns risk, which occurs after your accumulation years, which means it is of special significance to those preparing to retire and those who are newly retired.

The retirement philosophy I have outlined is based on finding the right investment products for the right retirement goals. Chapter 4 is about the investments themselves, looking at specific guaranteed and non-guaranteed products. I also break them down into the spheres of banks, brokerage and insurance.

Annuities are an insurance product, and I devote special attention to the different types of guaranteed income they provide in Chapter 5.

Anyone headed into retirement is going to need to look carefully at Social Security—what their payments can and can't solve in a broader retirement plan. In Chapter 6, I discuss the different ways—of which there are more than 500—to claim Social Security, looking especially at timing, spousal and survivor benefits and other factors that determine when and how to file.

Having a financial advisor who both knows what they're doing and is committed to finding strategies for your retirement goals can make the difference in a successful retirement versus one in which you run out of money (considered the baseline for "failing"). In

Chapter 7, I explain why independent advisors, that is to say those who are not encouraged by their employer to sell certain products, may be advantageous when it comes to planning your retirement. Independent versus "captive" advisors also have different commitments, licenses and legal standards which I will explain.

In my own practice, I put a lot of emphasis, perhaps more than other retirement advisors, on tax mitigation. Many people don't realize that your taxes may actually be higher in retirement due to rising government deficits and the higher rates that apply with disbursements from certain accounts and products. Chapter 8 is where I get into the nuts and bolts of how to potentially reduce your tax burden in retirement.

In Chapter 9, I'll discuss the importance of addressing issues concerning your estate as part of an overall financial plan. Essentially, an estate plan is a plan for distributing your assets after you pass away.

The "Life" in Retire for L.I.F.E.™ is not just a matter of emphasis for me, but a specific acronym I've developed in the years I've spent helping advisors plan the retirement strategies of hundreds of clients. It stands for the four different buckets that I call Liquid, Income, Future and Estate: L.I.F.E. I'll discuss these concepts in Chapter 10.

Successful retirement planning is a combination of the philosophy that financial tools fit into a holistic plan with significant goals, rather than the other way around, and practicing the philosophy in concrete circumstances. What works for one client may not be so good for another because we are all different people with different goals. What I can't tell you in these pages is exactly how to plan your retirement, which is highly personal. By the time you finish reading this book you will know enough about the philosophy and process of retirement planning to hopefully give you confidence, with the help of a qualified advisor, to organize the junk drawer and figure out what products or tools will help you fix the retirement home of your future.

CHAPTER 2

RETIREMENT RISKS

THERE'S no doubt that investing is always a risky proposition. However, when it comes to retirement investing, risks are magnified because you must live for an unknown number of years on the savings you accumulated during your working years. Retirement can last 20 or 30 years or longer and is a period in which you will lack the paycheck that you've depended on during your career. That means retirement investing requires close attention to the various risks involved.

When it comes to retirement income planning, those within the lowest income brackets may experience difficulties in terms of their plans failing. This means they run out of money before they die or must significantly cut back on their lifestyle if they don't have enough saved. Your chances of success may increase as you go up the income ladder. However, that doesn't mean that a positive outcome is guaranteed.

Why do these plans fail? Because of risks, which those retirees and their advisors fail to manage in a proactive manner. Risks are what this chapter is about. There are many of them, including sequence of returns risk, longevity risk, healthcare risk, long-term care risk, inflation risk and market volatility risk.

These risks cannot only be difficult to manage one at a time, but they can also combine to elevate your overall risks in retirement. Think about what might happen if inflation spikes at the same time you or your partner needs long-term care. Or, the market tanks right after you retire, producing sequence of returns risk, at the same time you or your partner has a health issue.

The point of holistic retirement income planning is to create a stream of income while growing your remaining savings to cope with these risks, however they may present themselves during retirement. Without careful planning, any one of these risks can negatively impact retirement—in combination, they are potentially devastating. This chapter goes over these risks and why they must be addressed. In future chapters, I'll present mitigation strategies so they don't take your retirement down.

SEQUENCE OF RETURNS RISK

Because sequence of returns risk is such a significant risk, Chapter 3 covers this risk in depth. Here's a preview of the information in that chapter. You already know that the market fluctuates. Sequence of risk returns occurs when you retire during a period of market decline. Alternatively, you could run into a market decline shortly after you retire.

Once you retire, you are "locked in" to having to experience whatever returns the market is providing. Specifically, sequence of returns risk involves the potential that you will retire during a period of market decline or that you will experience a market decline early on in your retirement, which can permanently damage your retirement income portfolio and the income you can generate from that portfolio.

Sequence refers to the order of market returns in the market, whether they are up and down. The risk that you might experience negative returns early during these periods can mean that your income will be reduced or the period your money will last is reduced. Those losses are then compounded by the need to take additional money out of the portfolio to pay for your living expenses during retirement.[1]

A good advisor will talk to you first about choosing the best date to retire in their opinion, without being able to see into the future. There is only so much that can be done to control sequence of returns risk from the retirement date point of view. In Chapter 3, you'll learn more about sequence of return risk and approaches to minimize it, including annuities that provide ongoing income in retirement regardless of the performance of the market.

LONGEVITY RISK

No one ever knows how long they will live, although actuarial science offers predictions with some degree of probability. Recall earlier that we defined retirement plan failure as outliving your own assets. Therefore, longevity risk describes the instance in which your actual survival rate and life expectancy exceeds that of your savings.[2]

What is life expectancy? Actuaries calculate it as the highest probable age of a man or woman born in a certain year. But there are all kinds of other factors including race, income, geographical location and so on to consider. In retirement planning, we look most at the life expectancy at attained age. For instance, if you are age 65 when you retire, how long can you expect to live? And there are all kinds of complications, many based on health—for example, if you smoke, or used to, and how long.

At its best, life expectancy at attained age is a guess. It's a median number, and you can't count on being in the population that, at age 65, could expect to live to age 88 just based on the charts. Research shows that 43 percent of retirees underestimate their life expectancy by at least five years.[3]

Americans are living longer today due to better medical technologies.[4] The best strategy for controlling longevity risk is to have a conservative planning horizon—looking at the very outside limit of how long you will live.[5] That means you don't want to underestimate your life expectancy. It can be better to over-estimate your life expectancy and end up with extra income or savings that you can leave to your heirs than underestimate your life expectancy and run short on income and savings.

Playing it safe means that you and your financial advisor can control spending levels over different stages of retirement today, so you have the money later down the road for the outsized expenses of healthcare and long-term care, which we'll get to immediately.

HEALTHCARE RISK

It's no news to anyone that older people get sick more and retired people are usually older. Keeping in mind our earlier definitions of success and failure, healthcare risk to a retirement plan is the risk that healthcare costs could come on suddenly in an emergency situation or over time, through rising prescription costs, or through copays involved in a long-term illness, and will whittle down your retirement savings to nothing.

While most seniors who retire have Medicare to cover many of the costs of healthcare, that still may not be enough, especially considering how much healthcare has inflated in cost over the years—4.22% per year, which exceeds the general rate and the cost-of-living adjustment to Social Security as well.[6]

You also need to consider that Medicare doesn't cover many expenses, including long-term care, hearing aids, dental care, dentures, eye exams, glasses and contacts, and routine foot care.[7] On average, people spend more than $5,000 out of pocket annually—or more than $400 per month—on their Medicare costs, according to the Kaiser Family Foundation (KFF).

Rising healthcare costs and Medicare coverage gaps are very serious challenges that form an important part of minimizing healthcare risk. According to Fidelity, a 65-year-old heterosexual married couple retiring in 2021 can expect to spend $300,000 on healthcare in retirement. Single men can expect $143,000, and single women, $157,000. This has risen 30% from 2011 and 88% since 2002, when measurements began.[8] HealthView Services estimated in March 2021 that the same healthy 65-year-old couple who collect Social Security at that age could expect healthcare costs to consume 68% of their benefits.[9]

Longer lifespans and rising prescription costs are just two of the main reasons for this increase. Medicare will step in to cover some, but not all of these costs. Furthermore, many seniors retire before age 65, which is when you become eligible for Medicare.[10]

Concretely, older people are more susceptible to chronic health conditions and diseases like arthritis, diabetes, and heart disease or failure. Up to 80% of them have at least one chronic condition. These limit your ability to perform daily tasks and may lead to long-term care needs. Moreover, they are among the leading causes of death in older adults in and of themselves. A sudden event, especially a fall, can lead to injury, hospitalization, rehab and premature death. That does not even to take into account the needs for behavioral or mental health, and oral health as well.[11]

LONG-TERM CARE RISK

Healthcare risk is intrinsically connected to long-term care risk since the most chronic illnesses require long-term care.[12] Long-term care insurance does exist, and some retirees have had the foresight to purchase it. Among those who do, some own policies with premiums that increase over the years.

The danger is you get older, and just at the point you might need that long-care benefit in the immediate future, you can't afford it if premiums rise too much. At that point, when the worst happens, you will either be forced to draw down the assets you need for the rest of your life or rely on loved ones to take care of you either personally or to sign the checks. From my perspective as a financial advisor, retirement income plans should proactively plan for this expense so that you mitigate this risk as much as possible.

Long-term care may be divided for the sake of convenience into home care, care in a temporary rehabilitation facility, or in a nursing-home-style facility, which is likely to be permanent for many. While Medicare covers many rehabilitation or short-term stays, it does not cover long-term care. However you slice it, long-term care is a rising need and hence a rising cost. According to the Administration for Community Living of the Department of Health and Human Services, more than two-thirds of those currently at age 65 and older will need it at some point in their lives.[13] And while, again, many people expect Medicare to pitch in for this, it does cover care not beyond rehabilitation stays. This is something that every future retiree must consider carefully, especially with the potential to develop serious chronic diseases such as dementia.[14]

Dementia one of those worst-case, end-of-life scenarios. But in retirement you can imagine many less worse case scenarios, like breaking a hip and the care you would need then. Consider how much you can rely on savings, family and insurance. Long-term care risk is one of the biggest risks that retirees face, which is why it is so important to plan for it proactively.

INFLATION RISK

We all have the vague idea that inflation means increase in the cost of goods and services but may know next to nothing about what it means concretely, which leaves us grasping at ends when we consider how it impacts our plans for retirement.

If you've been following how we define each of the risks in this chapter, then you could probably foresee that inflation risk means that the prices of the things we need will be greater than what we have saved once we hit retirement. We've already mentioned that costs of healthcare, which include long-term care, tend to rise faster than the general inflation rate, which is an important thing to keep in mind since these weigh heavy during the years of retirement. So even when inflation in general is low, retirees will be hit by it harder than others.[15]

Increasing lifespans means that the time people spend in retirement is longer. A married couple, or for that matter, a single person who in the past might have lived until their mid-80s after retiring at 65, might well be living until 90, 95 or even 100 or past that.[16] Consider that with a modest inflation rate of around 3%, leaving aside the spiraling costs under the rubric of healthcare which rise faster than the official rate, spending on day-to-day cost of living from when you retire at 65 to 89 will double.[17]

The Consumer Price Index says that prices have risen 5% or more for three consecutive months, and even if goes down, it probably won't go below the 2.9% which has been the average for the past decade. And even a temporary spike in inflation slows the growth of your retirement savings and crimps it especially should you be unlucky enough to retire when it's happening.[18]

One way, which I'll discuss in later chapters, to mitigate inflation is to position a certain part of your assets, which you don't need for income, to grow in the market. This can help you keep up with inflation, especially rising costs from taxes and healthcare/long-term care.

MARKET VOLATILITY RISK

Market volatility is a risk that is key to the first risk that I touched on in this chapter, sequence of returns risk. Under sequence of returns risk, you're looking at the possibility that the market might negatively impact your whole retirement strategy from the beginning. Market volatility risk means the risk that the market will fluctuate during your retirement, potentially under-performing the rates that you need to sustain the growth portion of your portfolio.

VOLATILITY: INCOME RISKS*

Return needed to break even after an income loss when in the "accumulation" phase:

% LOSS	% GAIN TO GET BACK TO EVEN
10%	11.1%
20%	25%
30%	42.9%
50%	100%

Return needed to break even in three years after a loss with 4% annual withdrawals when in the "distribution" phase:

% LOSS	% GAIN TO GET BACK TO EVEN
10%	26%
20%	42%
30%	63%
50%	321%

*http://www.morganstanleyfa.com/public/facilityfiles/sb070213121949/a9
9d1de4-ac8f-4d9b-a1e6-4f047831ab29.pdf
This is a hypothetical example provided for illustrative purposes only; it does
not represent a real-life scenario and should not be construed as advice
designed to meet the particular needs of an individual's situation.

As in the case of sequence of returns risk, there's no way to see with a crystal ball what may or may not happen in the market at any defined point during your retirement. But there are predictors of how long good and bad periods in the market last, and intelligent economists have predicted the best behavior based on that. A bear market occurs every 3.6 years on average and lasts about 9.6 months (9 months and 18 days). Compared to this, a bull market, which is the normal condition, lasts for about 2.7 years—973 days.[19]

Retirement investing is not like investing when you're younger. It's about protecting what you have, not trying to shoot for the highest possible rate of return. Still, even the common sense of a conservative investment strategy tells us that we should have the discipline to stick to the plan we set out at the beginning of retirement, even if a crash may incline us to do otherwise.[20] History tells us we will be rewarded. Not only are stock market downturns typically followed by a longer period of positive performance—since 1987, but every major decline in US equities has also been reversed by between 21%-68%, within the following year.[21]

The worst strategy for a retiree during a financial crash may be that they withdraw from the market. When you pull out money when the market's down and inflation continues to rise, there's extra pressure to maintain your income and lifestyle which, because you pulled out your money already, there's no longer the resources to do. Our approach is that clients should stay steady and stick to their plan. It can be difficult to stick with a well-designed plan when the market news is screaming in your ear that you should sell.[22]

CHAPTER 3

SEQUENCE OF RETURNS RISK

IN THE LAST CHAPTER, you learned about the various financial risks that can be encountered in retirement planning. Some of them, like inflation and market volatility, aren't exactly unique to financial planning for retirees. However, in retirement they take on an exaggerated form because you have much less margin for error than when you're still working. Healthcare, long-term care, longevity risk and the like are central to retirement and therefore much of our planning has to account for these issues.

Sequence of returns is a type of risk that falls primarily on those preparing to retire and newly retired. In this chapter we'll do a deeper dive into the meaning of sequence of returns risk to show why it is so significant and how planning can resolve what would otherwise be a huge obstacle to a prosperous and happy retirement.

WHAT IS SEQUENCE OF RETURNS RISK?

Following up on what I mentioned in the last chapter, sequence of returns risk is the risk of having negative returns at the point that the market will decline just before your retirement or right after you retire. Before I get into that, it's important to understand that your average rate of return doesn't change how the market has performed over a certain time period. You can put the returns in any order, and you'll still have the same value at the end of the period. Essentially, sequence of returns doesn't matter until you start taking withdrawals. Once the withdrawals happen, the rate at which the value decreases is greater when the returns are negative in the early years of the same time period.

With this baseline, you can see how if this occurs, it could dramatically raise the chance that you will run out of money in retirement. This can happen when you start drawing down income from your retirement savings at a time when those savings have diminished in value. This means that you're taking money out of an account that has depreciated in value and that your withdrawals will also comprise a larger portion of your overall savings.

According to Wade Pfau, PhD, professor of Retirement Income at the American College of Financial Services, sequence of returns is "the heightened vulnerability individuals face regarding the realized investment portfolio returns in the years around their retirement."[1] He goes on to say that retiring at the start of a bear market is exceptionally dangerous because your wealth can be depleted quickly as you are forced to withdraw more from a portfolio that's diminishing in value.[2]

Sequence of returns risk is related to ordinary investment/market volatility risk—which I explored some in the last chapter—but this risk has a much more significant impact on your investment portfolio in retirement than it does when you are not taking withdrawals. This is because with a bad early sequence, you are so to speak "locked in" to a pattern of growth that depletes your investments early, and later on there is less potential to recover. However, prior to retirement or taking withdrawals, you have the opportunity to bounce back from market volatility or a bear market, because you are still contributing to your savings and have time to ride out the bad sequence.

It's important to note that you don't have to encounter an all-out financial meltdown at the time of your retirement, like what happened in 1929 or even 2008, to experience sequence of returns risk. Even a stalling or slight dip in the market at the time you retire can still imperil your income in retirement.[3]

The pattern or sequence is that early in or close to retirement, the market takes a big hit, or a smaller hit that still affects your portfolio significantly. This forces you to take out money from the portfolio to live on in the early and intermediate years of retirement. We know in advance, without the benefit of any crystal ball, that inflation, health-care and long-term care risks can weigh more heavily on older retirees, as discussed in Chapter 2. The money you needed for that, by the time you get there, might have already been spent.[4] Even if that doesn't happen, there is a strong potential for a reduction in income to prevent this occurrence, which means that you'll have to reduce your lifestyle at a time when your costs are rising.

ANNIE, EMPLOYEE: SEQUENCE OF RETURNS

Figure 1 demonstrates the sequence of market returns that occurred from 2000-2022 without any withdraws that would typically occur in retirement. For an employee like Annie, who had contributed $100,000 to her 401(k) plan by 2000 and invested it in the stock market, the negative sequences that occurred between 2000-2002 and in 2008 and 2017 were not unduly significant. Annie, who was still working, was able to ride out these negative market movements, ultimately ending up with a balance of $261,978. Ideally, Annie would continue contributing to her 401(k) plan; however, for illustration purposes, this example is easier to understand.

FIGURE 1*

Year	Beginning Balance	Historical Return	Annual Withdrawal
2000	100,000	-10.1%	0
2001	89,861	-13.0%	0
2002	78,141	-23.4%	0
2003	59,882	26.4%	0
2004	75,679	9.0%	0
2005	82,486	3.0%	0
2006	84,961	13.6%	0
2007	96,532	3.5%	0
2008	99,939	-38.5%	0
2009	61,477	23.5%	0
2010	75,896	12.8%	0
2011	85,597	0.0%	0
2012	85,595	13.4%	0
2013	97,069	29.6%	0
2014	125,803	11.4%	0
2015	140,133	-0.7%	0
2016	139,115	9.5%	0
2017	152,379	19.4%	0
2018	181,971	-7.0%	0
2019	169,216	30.4%	0
2020	220,714	16.1%	0
2021	256,277	26.9%	0
2022	325,197	-19.4%	0
TOTAL	261,978	4.3%	0

*This is a hypothetical example provided for illustrative purposes only; it does not represent a real-life scenario and should not be construed as advice designed to meet the particular needs of an individual's situation.

BILL, RETIREE: SEQUENCE OF RETURNS

Figure 2 shows the same sequence of market returns, except this time the savings is needed for income in retirement. The withdrawals of $4,000 a year show the impact of a 4% withdrawal rate on the initial stock market portfolio of $100,000. For a retiree like Bill, sequence of returns risk, which occurred at the very beginning of his retirement, was disastrous. Immediately, within the first three years, the value of Bill's portfolio fell from $100,000 to $70,662 due to an adverse sequence of -10.1%, -13% and -23.4%.

The account balance also fell because of the $4,000 withdrawals due to the income that Bill needed in his retirement. Retirees like Bill, who are dependent upon their investment portfolio, are in a difficult position when they experience these adverse sequence events.

| FIGURE 2* | | | |
Year	Beginning Balance	Historical Return	Annual Withdrawal
2000	100,000	-10.1%	4,000
2001	85,861	-13.0%	4,000
2002	70,662	-23.4%	4,000
2003	50,151	26.4%	4,000
2004	59,381	9.0%	4,000
2005	60,722	3.0%	4,000
2006	58,544	13.6%	4,000
2007	62,518	3.5%	4,000
2008	60,724	-38.5%	4,000
2009	33,354	23.5%	4,000
2010	37,177	12.8%	4,000
2011	37,929	0.0%	4,000
2012	33,928	13.4%	4,000
2013	34,476	29.6%	4,000
2014	40,682	11.4%	4,000
2015	41,315	-0.7%	4,000
2016	37,015	9.5%	4,000
2017	36,545	19.4%	4,000
2018	39,642	-7.0%	4,000
2019	32,863	30.4%	4,000
2020	38,864	16.1%	4,000
2021	41,126	26.9%	4,000
2022	48,186	-19.4%	4,000
TOTAL	34,819	1.6%	88,000

*This is a hypothetical example provided for illustrative purposes only; it does not represent a real-life scenario and should not be construed as advice designed to meet the particular needs of an individual's situation.

BILL, RETIREE: A DIFFERENT SEQUENCE OF RETURNS

Figure 3 illustrates how a different sequence of returns during this 22-year period between 2000 and 2022 would have had an even worse impact on Bill's portfolio. For example, if Bill had retired in 2008 instead of 2000, his portfolio would have immediately taken a -38.5% hit along with the $4,000 withdrawal, reducing his balance in one year from $100,000 to $57,000. Ouch! If Bill experienced this sequence of returns, his future would have been even more bleak than in Figure 2, reducing his overall balance to a mere $8,027 by his 20th year of retirement.

FIGURE 3*

Year	Beginning Balance	Historical Return	Annual Withdrawal
2008	100,000	-38.5%	4,000
2021	57,514	26.9%	4,000
2014	68,981	11.4%	4,000
2002	72,839	-23.4%	4,000
2018	51,819	-7.0%	4,000
2005	44,187	3.0%	4,000
2019	41,513	30.4%	4,000
2003	50,147	26.4%	4,000
2001	59,376	-13.0%	4,000
2012	47,632	13.4%	4,000
2017	50,017	19.4%	4,000
2004	55,730	9.0%	4,000
2007	56,742	3.5%	4,000
2020	54,745	16.1%	4,000
2011	59,566	0.0%	4,000
2013	55,564	29.6%	4,000
2009	68,012	23.5%	4,000
2010	79,964	12.8%	4,000
2016	86,185	9.5%	4,000
2000	90,403	-10.1%	4,000
2022	77,237	-19.4%	4,000
2006	58,222	13.6%	4,000
2015	62,151	-0.7%	4,000
TOTAL	57,700	2.6%	88,000

*This is a hypothetical example provided for illustrative purposes only; it does not represent a real-life scenario and should not be construed as advice designed to meet the particular needs of an individual's situation.

These examples show how big of an advantage workers have when it comes to sequence of returns over retirees. Workers have the time to ride out market volatility and sequence of returns, whereas retirees have no such luxury.

WHEN TO WORRY ABOUT SEQUENCE OF RETURNS

In my practice, I've developed a rule of thumb that goes like this: Up to five years before your retirement, you still have the luxury of time to ride out sequence of returns risk. Between when you start working and five years before your retirement can be the timeframe for taking advantage of market volatility to grow your savings because you don't have to worry about sequence of returns risk.

However, once you enter that period of five years before retirement, you may consider pulling back on the risk in your retirement investment portfolio to mitigate the sequence of returns risk. I refer to this as the preservation phase, where you're primarily seeking to preserve your current assets over building significantly on them, and hence your strategy must be more conservative. The third phase, distribution, is of course retirement itself.

I set the divider between accumulation and preservation at five years from retirement because of market volatility risk. At no point in time historically, even during the worst recession, have investors who bought and held their assets not recouped their losses over the ensuing five-year period.[5] So, while there is no crystal ball that reveals when the market is going to stall or crash, the five-year divider between accumulation and preservation effectively controls for what is otherwise a highly dangerous risk to retirement assets.

What this means is that five years from retirement should mark the point when you and your financial advisor should be paying close attention to what's happening in the market, looking out for that stall or bear and adjusting your strategy accordingly. You don't have to or want to risk the assets you need to retire on in the preservation phase —and definitely not in the distribution phase.

Any retirement planner worth their salt will discuss sequence of returns risk with their clients early in their relationship. The sad fact is that many advisors only plan for accumulation, rather than preservation and distribution. Regardless of how old you are, you will likely retire one day, so it's important to choose an advisor who is aware of these risks and who will plan for them in your retirement income plan.

THE EFFICIENT FRONTIER

A strategy that achieves the desired amount of income in retirement balanced against an acceptable amount of risk to assets is called "the efficient frontier" of retirement planning. While you are, of course, in charge of your own risk tolerance, your retirement income plan should take this efficient frontier into account.

The typical goal of retirement planning is not to get extremely rich or achieve great wealth but to guarantee that you'll have enough income to pay your essential expenses without having to draw down your other assets. Market volatility risk, as I described, is what happens when the market takes a hit, and a wrench is thrown into the gears of your retirement plan which is hard for you or even the most expert mechanic to get out. Hence the five-year rule, and hence the division between accumulation, preservation and distribution phases of retirement investing.

The way advisors deal with market volatility risk is the Monte Carlo simulation. This goes together with the mindset of planning for accumulation over preservation and distribution. So, they will run a simulation that shows there is "only" a 10-15% chance of failure with a given established plan.

First, a simulation can tell us only so much, and it's unfortunate that many advisors will exclusively rely on them to predict likelihood of failure. They do this because a Monte Carlo simulation sounds like it has magical powers, is precise and accurate, which they can dress up further using fancy language.

Second, the 10-15% risk of failure to me is too much. For many investors there is no reason to keep that much risk on the table, even assuming that everything is right with the simulation and the risk is fairly small. You never have to, and definitely shouldn't want to, put yourself in a position that could lead to running out of money in retirement. That advice goes for even the wealthiest client with the best financial advisor who has the most sophisticated simulation.

I've been in the unfortunate position of having to tell clients that they must cut back on their lifestyle during retirement because they are in danger of running out of money. It is a task that I never, ever want to engage in again. You deserve an advisor who will do every-thing in their power to ensure that you have sufficient income in retirement through guaranteed* income vehicles such as fixed index annuities, which we will discuss in future chapters.

Guarantees provided by annuities are subject to the financial strength of the issuing insurance company; not guaranteed by any bank or the FDIC. Guaranteed lifetime income available through annuitization or the purchase of an optional lifetime income rider, a benefit for which an annual premium is charged.

MOVING FORWARD

In Chapter 4, you'll learn about different types of products, both guaranteed and non-guaranteed. Those with guaranteed values include savings accounts, certificates of deposit, fixed index annuities and life insurance. Investments that aren't guaranteed include stocks, bonds, mutual funds, exchange-traded funds, real estate investment trusts and variable annuities. Later in the book, I'll explain how to use both of these types of products to achieve a balanced retirement income plan that will provide income while protecting you against risks.

CHAPTER 4

TWO TYPES OF INVESTMENTS

ALL INVESTMENTS IN THE WORLD, from owning a savings account to a hefty amount of stock in a big blue-chip company, can be divided into guaranteed money and non-guaranteed money. The central difference for you to grasp as a retirement investor is that guaranteed money will not lose or gain value on the principal, while non-guaranteed money or investments can and do.

To quote the expert definition, "non-guaranteed income (or money or investments) is anything that's subject to market changes and are not guaranteed to last a certain amount of time. Guaranteed income, on the other hand, is fixed and structured for a certain amount of time and can even be designed to last a lifetime."[1]

In this chapter, I'll talk about why sound retirement planning requires a mix of guaranteed and non-guaranteed money, investments and income. You should never have all your eggs in one or the other basket, because both types of products have potential upsides and downsides, the greater or lesser depending on the specific type of product involved.

Therefore, I'll be going into specific detail about some types of guaranteed money, including checking and savings accounts, money market accounts, fixed index annuities and life insurance, as well as non-guaranteed money which includes stocks, bonds, and the products derived from them like mutual funds and exchange-traded funds, as well as variable annuities and real estate investment trusts. As a financial advisor with a great deal of experience in helping retirees and future retirees plan their future, I have specific reasons why I like some instruments and dislike others, which I'll explain as I go.

TYPES OF GUARANTEED MONEY

Checking accounts are used to manage day-to-day finances. You may have your paycheck automatically deposited into a checking account and then use those funds to pay your bills. You can open a checking account at a bank, savings and loan or credit union, either at an institution that has actual brick and mortar branches or those that are online only. Checking accounts are guaranteed by the FDIC up to $250,000 and are highly liquid, meaning you have access to your money any time.[2]

Savings accounts exist for the purpose of maintaining an emergency fund or saving for big ticket items like a car or vacation. You may allocate money to your savings through payroll deduction or through transfers from your checking account. Like checking accounts, savings accounts are available at banks, savings and loans, and credit unions. Your savings are guaranteed by the FDIC up to $250,0000 and are available at any time.[3] Certain accounts offer a modest interest rate on your money but require higher minimum balances. Regular savings accounts generally offer miserly interest rates.

Money market accounts offer higher interest rates but require higher minimum balances than traditional savings accounts. They are also covered by the FDIC as with banks, savings and loans, and credit unions. There's a difference between money market accounts and money market funds. Money market funds aren't covered by the FDIC and are offered by brokerage, asset management and other financial services organizations.

Certificates of Deposit (CDs) require locking up your money for a period of time, usually anywhere from six months to five years. They are offered by banks and credit unions and are also covered by the FDIC. A CD may be suitable for you if you're willing to lock up your money in return for a higher interest rate.

Money market funds are offered by mutual fund companies, brokerages and other financial services firms. They pool short-term investments together to offer liquid accounts associated with open-ended checking, deposit and withdrawal privileges. Unlike money market accounts, money market funds aren't covered by the FDIC. While money market funds usually maintain a stable value, during the financial crisis a major money market fund "broke the buck," which refers to the $1 per share value that they typically maintain. However, the U.S. government bailed out the banks so that shareholders didn't lose any money.[4]

Fixed index annuities are insurance contracts sold by insurance companies in which you put down a certain amount of money in exchange for payouts over a term set between you and the company. A fixed index annuity is so called because the interest credits, if any, are based on the performance of an underlying index such as the S&P 500. These products are attractive for pre-retirees and retirees because they offer consistent income, provide principal protection in a down market and upside potential in rising markets. The fixed index annuities product has certain levers that limit interest credits based on the upside performance of the index. In many of the products, there is the potential to withdraw up to 10% of your principal each year. Fixed index annuities are otherwise considered an illiquid product. You can withdraw more than 10% but you will be charged an early withdrawal penalty. That's why it's important to understand the role of a fixed index annuity in your portfolio before you buy one.[5]

Life insurance is designed to provide funds for your heirs when you pass away. Generally, life insurance is more suitable to those with young children, although survivor's benefits can come in handy for a retired surviving spouse. However, I generally prefer other retirement products when it comes to providing income in retirement. That's because maintaining a life insurance policy, especially a whole life policy, requires ongoing premiums. Instead of paying these premiums, it may make sense to buy a product such as a fixed index annuity to provide income in retirement.

NON-GUARANTEED MONEY

Stocks represent partial ownership in a publicly traded company. When you buy stock in a company, you have the right to vote on important matters at the company's annual meeting and to participate in the value the company creates. That value fluctuates in the public markets, depending on fundamental factors related to the company itself as well as outside factors such as the economy as a whole, interest rates and so forth. Stock prices fluctuate and therefore represent non-guaranteed money. Some companies pay dividends to shareholders. A dividend is a payment of cash or stock that usually occurs on a quarterly basis. There are many different kinds of companies issuing publicly traded stock. Some are large multi-national companies while others are small companies that operate in one country. While stocks are risky, they also offer the potential to grow and increase your investment. Investing in stocks in retirement can help mitigate risks such as inflation, healthcare and longevity.

Bonds are a type of debt issued by a company or a government. Typically, bonds are issued for a set period of time. During this period of time, the entity that issues the bond pays you interest, usually twice a year. When the bond matures, you get your principal back. Bonds vary in terms of their safety. Among the safest bonds are U.S. government bonds.[6] Bonds from some of the largest and most stable U.S. and international corporations are also highly regarded. Then there are bonds from less financially stable companies or countries that are considered riskier. The riskier the perception of the issuing entity, the higher the interest rate that the issuer must pay to sell their bonds. That means, for example, that rates on U.S. government bonds are much lower than small, less financially stable companies. In the early 1980s, bonds began to fall from very high rates to the extremely low rates that have prevailed since the 2007-09 financial crisis.[7][8] These low rates mean that it is very difficult to earn sufficient income in retirement from investing in bonds. In fact, investing in government bonds may not even keep pace with inflation.

Mutual funds are pooled investments of stocks, bonds and other types of assets. There are thousands of mutual funds based on a variety of investment styles and preferences, including bond funds, stock funds and funds composed of both stocks and bonds. The major fund categories are index funds, or passively managed funds, which track a market index such as the S&P 500 and actively managed funds, which are based on a specific methodology designed to outperform specific market indexes. Mutual funds carry fees such as the management fee and the expense ratio. They also have many other types of fees that are difficult to determine that can inflate your costs.

Exchange-traded funds (ETFs) are a pooled investment vehicle closely related to mutual funds. Like mutual funds, there are many different types of ETFs, although most are passively rather than actively managed. The major difference between mutual funds and ETFs is that ETFs are traded on the stock exchanges rather than sold through brokers, financial services companies and asset management firms. ETFs typically have lower fees. You can also buy and sell them at any time when the markets are open in contrast to mutual funds, which can only be bought or sold at the end of a trading day.

Real estate investment trusts (REITs): Think of REITs as a relative of the mutual fund or exchange-traded fund that deals specifically in real estate, making and returning money based on the space they lease and rent out. If you are invested in a mutual or exchange-traded fund, you might already be invested in an REIT as well. Compared to some, REITs are straightforward investments, investing in different types of property such as apartment buildings, offices, warehouses and shopping centers.[9] There are many different types of REITs–some buy all sorts of properties, while others specialize in certain types of property in specific regions of the country.

Variable annuities are contracts between you and an insurance company that makes periodic payments for a set term in a similar fashion to fixed index annuities. The main difference is in the payments and the fees—variable annuities do not guarantee a set payment, unliked fixed index annuities and they also charge much higher fees.[10] The payment goes up or down depending on the index they are based on.

IMPLICATIONS FOR RETIREMENT

Both guaranteed and non-guaranteed money have their advantages and disadvantages and also have a place in a retirement income plan. Guaranteed money is useful in terms of ensuring that you have enough income coming in to cover your basic expenses in retirement. This is an area where you don't want to mess around, because it is very stressful not knowing if you're going to be able to continue to pay your basic bills as you age. That's why I like guaranteed income products such as fixed index annuities that provide necessary income without a lot of fees. These products also offer upside potential and the ability to remove some principal if you have an emergency.

Research reveals that retirees with guaranteed income are both happier and live longer.[11] Why? It's obvious. If you don't need to worry about how to pay your basic living expenses–housing, healthcare and so on, you're freed up to enjoy life. No one retires "just in case" or to always be nervous about everything. It kind of defeats the purpose. If you're free of worry and financially comfortable, you're less likely to over- or under-spend, thus creating a virtuous circle which ends in a retirement well lived. This gives us good reasons to look into vehicles like a fixed index annuity when we have the chance.

Non-guaranteed money–specifically, money invested in the stock market–is also important because it facilitates growth that can help mitigate risks such as high healthcare costs, living into your 90s or even to 100, inflation, and potentially rising taxes. How does money invested in the market help minimize these risks? Because that money, over the long term, is likely to increase in value so that you will eventually have more assets to deal with these risks as they arise.

Also, it is much easier to be relaxed about stock market fluctuations when you have your expenses already covered by guaranteed income. For example, if the market falls by 20 percent in the year that you turn 75, you won't be inclined to freak out because you know that your expenses are already covered by your fixed income annuity payments. With that in mind, you can just let what you've invested in the stock market recover–as it has always done in the past–confident that your income needs are already taken care of by another part of your retirement income portfolio.

Covering your needs for income, growth and risk mitigation with a portfolio combined of guaranteed and non-guaranteed money is the best recipe for retirement success in my opinion. That way, you won't be risking your income in the stock market, and you also won't be tying up your assets too conservatively with too much guaranteed money. In fact, I believe in strategies that use only the required amount to generate income to cover your bills and then investing the rest in the stock market for growth to cope with the variety of risks discussed in Chapter 3.

Let's talk about a hypothetical couple named Jim and Betsy who have $1 million in retirement savings. Of that total, we take 30% or $300,000 to purchase a fixed index annuity to guarantee them enough income. The rest of their retirement savings–70% or the other $700,000–is invested in the stock market based on their risk tolerance, reinvesting their dividends for the future. This way, they have a retirement income portfolio balanced appropriately between income and growth. That's a couple that has a good chance of reaching the virtuous circle of retirement investment. With the right tools and planning, it's an outcome I aim to provide to all of my clients, however much they have saved and whatever their preferences.

Unfortunately, there are other advisors who may have gone all or nothing with that portfolio. If they had worked with an insurance agent who only sold insurance and annuities, that agent could have put all their money into a fixed index or even a variable annuity. That would have given them more income than they needed and exposed them to the risks I discussed in Chapter 3. They would have had a higher risk profile because the annuity or annuities would not have provided them with enough growth to counter inflation, longevity, healthcare expenses and more.

Or, they might have worked with a broker who may have put a higher percentage of their retirement into the stock market. That could have meant little or no guaranteed income and exposure to market volatility. Can you imagine how worried Betsy and Jim would have been if the market dropped 20 percent or more, which could have cost them $200,000 out of their nest egg? Over-investing in the stock market in retirement without sufficient guaranteed income is a recipe for a stressful, not a peaceful, retirement.

UP NEXT

In Chapter 5, I'll take a deep dive into annuities. You'll learn more about the different types of annuities and how to employ them in a retirement income portfolio.

CHAPTER 5

ANNUITIES 101

AS YOU LEARNED in Chapter 4, annuities are a product that provides ongoing income in retirement in exchange for a lump-sum payment. In this chapter, we take a deep dive into the various types of annuities and what they offer.

The four types of annuities that are most relevant for retirement are: single premium immediate annuities, variable annuities, fixed annuities and fixed index annuities. You can buy a plain vanilla annuity or an annuity with extra features, which in the annuity universe are known as riders.

It's important to note for retirement planning purposes that as a rule, once you sign an annuity contract, the money you use to purchase the annuity is no longer available for you to spend in other ways. In other words, annuities are not liquid assets. If, after signing an annuity contract, you need all or some of your money back, you will incur withdrawal penalties except under certain circumstances. For example, some annuity contracts allow you to withdraw 5 or 10% of your principal without penalty after the first year. However, withdrawing money from an annuity designed to give you retirement income defeats the whole purpose behind buying an annuity, which is to provide you with a certain amount of income for the rest of your life.

Of course, the benefits of handing over control of a certain amount of your retirement savings may outweigh the risks. But generally, we should see the money you put into an annuity as locked in for the rest of your life–it should be that in order to do the job we need it to do. That job is to provide the ongoing monthly income you need to pay your bills.

To that end, I'm going to describe the four types of annuities that can be used to create income in retirement.

SINGLE PREMIUM IMMEDIATE ANNUITIES

This is the most basic kind of annuity. With a single premium immediate annuity, once you sign the contract you start getting monthly payments for either a term that you select or your lifetime. The latter is the big one in retirement and that's mostly what I advise my clients to go for since none of us knows how long we're going to live.

The "immediate" part of a single premium immediate annuity means income starts within one year. There are deferred annuities that stay in an accumulation phase for longer than one year before distributing income at a later date.[1] Since it is deferred, this gives the account more time for potential growth and the payouts may be larger once you do start taking them.[2]

VARIABLE ANNUITIES

With a single premium immediate annuity contract, you know how much income you're going to be getting and when–it's a guarantee, for all practical purposes. A variable annuity changes all that. With a variable annuity, the premium you sign over to the insurance company can be divided into sub-accounts and invested in the market–usually mutual funds–that go up and down depending on market performance and hence determine a changing payout each month.

Variable annuities, like single premium immediate annuities, are meant to be held long term, and therefore count as retirement products. But since they depend on the market, the payout has no floor unlike other types of annuities. Variable annuities can be useful tools in some but not all circumstances due to these features.

FIXED ANNUITIES

A fixed annuity contract has a guaranteed, set interest rate which will not vary beyond the terms of the contract. According to the SEC, "The insurance company promises you a minimum rate of interest and a fixed amount of periodic payments."[3] The contrast to variable annuities could not be greater. The insurance company is required to provide interest and the value isn't affected by market declines.

FIXED INDEX ANNUITIES

Fixed index annuities–which are also known as index annuities–offer fixed monthly payments either through an income rider or annuitization. They differ from traditional fixed annuities in that there is the potential for increased interest credits based on the performance of an external index. The value of the contract may rise due to the performance of the index the annuity is based upon. One of the common indices for fixed index annuities is the S&P 500, an index of 500 of the largest and most successful companies in America.

If the index increases in value, you receive a credit to your contract value based on the performance of this external index. The index interest credits may also be calculated with a fee or participation rate that varies based on the terms of the contract. In other words, if the index does exceptionally well, you may be able to "participate" in these gains, although how much you participate is typically capped at a certain percentage. For example, if your participation rate in the S&P 500 index is capped at 10% and the index increases by 15% in one year, you will receive only 10% of that increase.

However, while many fixed index annuities limit your upside potential, they offer an important benefit on the downside. If the index has a down year and declines in value, your contract will not incur any losses due to the decline because there is no downside risk. This means that your contract can't decline in value due to market declines, which is very important in terms of preserving your principal and the income it generates for you to pay your bills in retirement.

Some annuity holders get confused when it comes to the value of their annuity. That's completely understandable because it can be a complex subject. There are several different types of values within a fixed index annuity. The annuity contract, issued by the insurance carrier defines these values. Below are some common definitions:

- Accumulation or account value: The current value of your annuity, which includes any interest, minus fees and withdrawals from your account.[4]
- Income benefit or income value: The income benefit value, which is separate from the other types of value, is the value that an income rider accumulates to over time.[5] I can't emphasize enough that the income value is not an actual value that you can cash out if you surrender the annuity. Instead, the income value is only used to determine the income payment you will receive from the income rider based on the terms of your contract.
- Annuity contract or cash surrender value: This is what your annuity is worth if you decide to surrender your annuity. If it is before the initial surrender period is over, the value would be the annuity's accumulation value minus surrender charges. At no time can it be less than the minimum guaranteed value.[6]

- Annuity contract or minimum guarantee value: This is the minimum amount that your contract is worth at any given time.

In many cases, I find that fixed index annuities can be a suitable product to provide guaranteed income in retirement for my clients. This is because of the features that allow the opportunity for some participation in market gains, protects you from market losses and guarantees income regardless of how long you live.

ANNUITY INCOME RIDERS

There are many different riders to annuity contracts, some of which I'll cover next. A rider on an annuity is an agreement added to the base contract at the time of purchase for a specific need. The rider costs are separate calculations in the contract that add to the overall cost of the contract. When you sign an annuity contract, it's important to go in knowing which riders you want because typically they can't be added afterwards.[7]

The first kind to know is an income rider. Typically, an income rider is an additional benefit to the contract that provides a guaranteed minimum withdrawal amount from the contract's value. Like other riders it's usually optional and carries an extra fee.

Look at it this way: The annuity income rider adds a lifetime payment to a fixed index annuity contract. Typically for a fee of 0-1% of the contract's value, you get a lifetime payment for yourself (and, if you want, your spouse) and you can keep control of the cash account. Meaning, if you pass away, your beneficiary gets whatever is left in the account. Alternatively, if you decide while you're still alive that you want to stop the annuity payments, the balance is still intact. Either way, you're covered because the income from the income rider is guaranteed to last your lifetime.

OTHER ANNUITY RIDERS

Some of the more common riders are:

- Death benefit riders guarantee an annual growth amount that can be used for legacy and estate planning. These can be especially important if your financial legacy is important to you and/or you don't qualify for straight life insurance.
- Long-term care riders, for an extra fee, set aside money that can be used for healthcare should you suffer a long-term illness either in an assisted living or rehabilitation facility or even at home. Many insurers consider that you qualify for the long-term illness payout if you cannot perform two out of the six activities of daily living (ADLs, these are typically eating, bathing, dressing, transferring, toileting, and continence).[8]
- Disability riders pay for the cost of care should you suffer a temporary or permanent disability, usually again linked to some portion of the ADLs.
- Terminal illness riders provide you instant access to your money, waiving the surrender charge should you be diagnosed with a terminal illness.

There are many other types of riders that are beyond the scope of this chapter. While riders outside of income guarantees can be useful, you also need to be careful because the costs involved in purchasing riders can add up and may cut into the income stream you need in retirement.

REASONS WHY GUARANTEEING INCOME IS IMPORTANT

My philosophy regarding annuities and guaranteed income is simple. I believe that it's important to guarantee enough income in retirement to pay your essential expenses. However, allocating too much of your savings to the guaranteed income bucket potentially limits the opportunity for growth therefore making it harder to mitigate other risks in retirement. A customized plan for retirement typically includes guaranteeing the minimum amount necessary to pay your essential expenses. Then, whatever is left can be invested in the market to grow over time. That growth will help you deal with many of the risks discussed in earlier chapters.

For example, if inflation spikes, over time, an increase in the value of your stock portfolio will help you deal with the issue of eroding purchasing power and rising prices. Investing in the market can also help mitigate longevity, healthcare and other risks. Annuities are a great tool for doing part of a necessary job in retirement–guaranteeing income–but they don't solve all problems in retirement. To deal with other problems, other tools such as stocks and vehicles that invest in stocks such as mutual funds and exchange-traded funds may be a better option.

NEXT UP

In Chapter 6, we move into the important subject of claiming Social Security and how it contributes to your retirement and your retirement income picture.

CHAPTER 6

CLAIMING SOCIAL SECURITY

WHEN I GIVE PRESENTATIONS, Social Security is one of the most popular topics. Many people have questions about the "right time" to claim Social Security benefits. It may sound like a typical salesman kind of answer, but I have to tell them this: *There is no correct, universal answer for any one person's specific situation. Everybody is a little bit different.*

Most people know that you can claim Social Security as early as age 62.[1] However, doing this comes with a substantial reduction in the benefits you'll receive over time compared to what you would receive if you waited until your full retirement age (FRA). Because of the reduction involved in claiming early, waiting until the FRA can be the best option for most people. Full retirement age is calculated based on your birth date. Once you reach age 70, you achieve the maximum benefit available, so at that point there's no real advantage in delaying any longer.[2]

Another question that surfaces frequently in my seminars is the future of Social Security. Millennials often wonder whether Social Security will be there when they retire.[3] They wonder whether they can count on the benefits that they see on their Social Security statements. Yes, there are certain limits to the trust funds linked to Social Security which, should they be exhausted, Social Security would have to pay reduced benefits.[4]

I do think that Social Security is such a popular program that both sides of the aisle should be able to come together to solve the deficit in the Social Security trust fund. Optimistically, retires could develop a plan that relies on more or less the same level of benefits being there for them.

SO, WHEN SHOULD I CLAIM?

Like I said, I don't like answering this question in my presentations. That's because I never can know the specific situation of the person asking it, as there are hundreds of different ways to claim Social Security.

The basic criteria for answering "when do I claim" is what financial advisors like myself call the break-even age. The break-even age is the "the point in your life when the total of those lower benefits is equal to the total benefits you would have received if you had waited to take your benefits at FRA, or even later."[5] For example, lots of people will want to claim Social Security at age 62, based on the assumption they won't live that long and there'll be no benefit to them in taking it later since they'll die before. I've found people typically underestimate how long they will live. The point in calculating the break-even age is that after this age–whatever it may be–is that you'll have received just as much in benefits as if you had claimed at age 62.[6]

There are various websites that'll tell you how to calculate your break-even age with Social Security, and should you be inclined, you could do it yourself in pen on the back of an envelope using your yearly Social Security statement that you can obtain by creating an account at www.ssa.gov.

But there's really no need to expend the effort or to incur the penalties that might come from making a math error. I have at my disposal sophisticated software that can instantly compare the hundreds of different ways of claiming and that will spit out a report telling you both your break-even age and when is best to claim based on added factors like your extra assets, any health problems or disabilities, at what age you plan to stop work, etc.

But let's get into specifics. You basically have four options when it comes to claiming:

1. Full retirement age, which is between ages 66 and 67, depending on when you were born.
2. Before your full retirement age, even as early as age 62.
3. Delay filing until age 70.
4. File after age 62 but before full retirement age or after full retirement age but before age 70.

Every person has something called a full retirement age or FRA. That's the earliest age at which you can file for Social Security and get your full benefit amount. If you were born between 1943 and 1954, your FRA is your 66th birthday. If you were born in 1960 or later, your FRA is your 67th birthday. If you were born from 1955 to 1959, your FRA is your 66th birthday plus two months for every year after 1954. For example, if you were born in 1956, your FRA is your 66th birthday plus four months.[7]

If you start at age 62 your benefit is reduced 30%, for life.[8] I have couples that come into my office and say they want to start Social Security at age 62 because they believe it's going to run out of money, and other people come in and say they want to wait until age 70 so they can get the highest benefit. Right now, according to the Social Security Administration, if the finances of the program aren't reworked, it is projected to only afford highly reduced payouts come 2035.

A complete retirement plan would include a strategy to obtain the most Social Security in your lifetime. Who wants the largest Social Security check? Now, who wants the most Social Security in their lifetime? The obvious answer is not always the right answer. I have software that will allow me to do a Social Security analysis based on your specific situation.

Another factor to consider, as I've mentioned, when deciding to start claiming your benefits is your "break-even" age. This is the age at which you come out ahead if you opt to delay receiving your benefits. Your break-even age will shift depending on the amount of your FRA benefits and the age at which you begin receiving Social Security.

If you're relatively healthy and have a history of longevity in your family, there's a greater likelihood that you'll reach your break-even age. Here's a simple calculation to give you an idea of how a Social Security break-even calculator works. Say that you have the option to begin receiving $1,200 a month in benefits at age 62. You'd receive $1,700 in benefits if you wait until full retirement age at 66. Or you could receive $2,200 a month in benefits by delaying until age 70.

The break-even point represents when the cumulative benefits even out. If you wait until age 70 to start taking benefits, it will take you until age 79 to break even with the benefit amount you'd receive if you started taking them at age 62. If you were to start receiving benefits at age 66, it would take you until age 75 to break even with the benefits you'd receive if you started them at age 62.

SPOUSAL BENEFITS

Social Security spousal benefits are another important aspect of Social Security. In my seminars, I get a lot of people asking how Social Security is affected by the strategy of claiming benefits based on the benefit that their predeceased spouse would have gotten—if they were married 10 years or more--and even more from divorced people, especially seeking to claim based on the benefit of a wealthier ex-partner who has paid more into the system. The good news is that these are both totally viable strategies for claiming, and that with a retirement financial planner like myself, we can sit down together, take these variables into account, and find the best strategy to work for you.

If you've been married for at least a year and your spouse has already claimed their benefits, you could still receive spousal benefits based on your spouse's work record once you reach age 62, even if you don't have a work history that qualifies you for your own benefits. The amount you'll receive in spousal benefits is determined by your own work record, the work record of your spouse, and the age at which you begin collecting spousal benefits. These spousal benefits can be worth up to 50 percent of your spouse's FRA benefits. As with individual benefits, if you begin receiving spousal benefits prior to your FRA, your benefits will be permanently reduced. One strategy to consider is to claim your own Social Security beginning at 62 and make the switch to spousal benefits when your husband or wife files.

When a Social Security beneficiary dies, his or her surviving spouse is eligible for survivor benefits. A surviving spouse can collect 100 percent of the late spouse's benefit if the survivor has reached full retirement age, but the amount will be lower if the deceased spouse claimed benefits before he or she reached full retirement age.[9] Full retirement age for survivor benefits differs from that for retirement and spousal benefits; it is currently 66 but will gradually increase to 67 over the next several years.[10]

Keep in mind that your ex-spouse doesn't have to currently be *receiving* Social Security benefits, they only have to be *eligible* to receive benefits. Claiming benefits based on your ex-spouse's record will have no effect on the benefits your ex-spouse will receive, and your ex-spouse is not notified if you choose to claim on their record. If your ex-spouse has remarried, your ex-spouse's new partner will also be eligible for spousal benefits.

However, you cannot take both retirement and spousal benefits *and* survivor benefits at the same time, so it's important to factor how each could impact your retirement income strategy so you want to make sure you are working with someone who is knowledgeable on this. I have this conversation with my clients all the time.[11]

WORKING AND BENEFITS

A key variable to consider in your claiming strategy is whether you are still working or not, even part-time. If you don't work any longer, then planning is mostly about determining your income based on your assets. But if you still have the capability to work and want to work for whatever reason, then from your FRA to age 70 you may not have the need to turn on Social Security and therefore get the full benefit. Benefits are changed based on how much you earn, up to the point at which you reach FRA.[12]

On the other hand, for some individuals who have reached their full retirement age and are still working, claiming Social Security early can position them to implement strategies such as Roth IRA Conversions. Those approaches can help offset the taxes involved in Roth IRA conversions implemented prior to age 72. Added income from work will also affect your break-even age for Social Security and the overall income strategy when deciding the best time to claim.

However, if you choose to work and claim Social Security before your full retirement age, there are earnings limits. If you exceed those earning limits, the government will take back some of your Social Security benefits. You will then receive a refund on those benefits once you achieve your full retirement age.

In 2022, the annual earnings limit for those claiming Social Security before the year in which they reach full retirement age is $19,590.[13] However, the earnings limit for the year in which you reach full retirement age is $51,960.[14]

Many people are unaware of the earnings limits and stunned when they find Social Security benefits they've already received getting clawed back by the government. That's why it's good to understand the earnings limits around claiming Social Security before full retirement age so you can make an intelligent decision as to whether it makes sense to work and claim prior to full retirement age.

FINDING YOUR PROVISIONAL INCOME

Up to 85% of your Social Security benefit can be liable for federal income taxes as ordinary income. This will happen if you have substantial income in addition to the benefit—wages or salary, which we just talked about, or interest and dividends from investments in addition to other income reported on your tax return.[15]

How much of it is actually taxed depends on your situation, and how much income you get from other sources. To find this out, we can calculate your provisional income, which is your adjusted gross income plus half your Social Security benefit, plus any additional income you received during the year. Based on this, the IRS might determine you owe taxes on anything from 50-85% of your benefit.[16] Fortunately, we have strategies like Roth conversion and others that limit the exposure of your benefit to taxation, which are again best hammered out in a meeting between a planner and client where both have all the information.

A FINAL WORD

As you can see, the universe of Social Security claiming is complex. By consulting with an experienced retirement income planner with sophisticated software, you can determine how Social Security fits into your retirement income situation and your break-even point.

In Chapter 7, you'll learn about the different types of financial advisors and which types are best to help you achieve your retirement income goals.

CHAPTER 7

FINANCIAL ADVISORS

SOMEONE WHO WALKS into my office for the first time won't likely know if I'm a "captive" or "independent" advisor or what that means, even though it is of foundational importance in terms of the approach I would take to their retirement income planning. In this chapter, you'll learn about the different kinds of financial advisors and licenses.

CAPTIVE VS. INDEPENDENT ADVISORS

The basic division between captive and independent advisors in the financial advisory world is based on the employer and the advisor's responsibilities and duties. What's called a "captive" advisor is a registered representative of the firm they work for—usually big firms like Edward Jones, Merrill Lynch or Morgan Stanley. Since they work for and represent only that firm, they are limited to recommend the investment products offered by their firm or those it offers on its platform.[1]

Compare this to an independent advisor. An independent financial advisor is associated with no firm other than their own practice and can offer products from an array of companies. They can look at many different products and strategies available to determine which is in the best interest of their client.[2]

One grey area is that there's an increasing number of large firms, that "franchise" and their advisors might use "John Smith Advisory Services" or some such language in their literature. But like owning a franchise of McDonald's still means you sell the Big Mac, a franchisee of one of these firms will still be selling the products limited to that much larger entity.[3]

True independence, which I practice as a fiduciary for my clients, is always in my view the best way to go. And since all financial advisors are required by the SEC to disclose their capabilities in this respect in clear and precise language in literature they provide to potential clients, there's no need for anyone to be confused or intimidated by this distinction.[4]

FINANCIAL ADVISORS AND/OR INSURANCE AGENTS

Another thing that can confuse potential clients is the difference between an investment advisor and an insurance agent. That's a real-world confusion which often crops up in my business since different kinds of insurance products like annuities are so often part of a comprehensive retirement strategy. Basically, while there are insurance agents and investment advisors, more and more people in my business are getting "dually licensed" which means they can sell both.

In terms of what we talked about in the previous section, many insurance agents are a lot like captive financial advisors—they are limited to those products sold and endorsed by the company they are employed by.[5] Some, however, are independent and can sell annuities, insurance and other insurance products from a variety of companies. However, regardless of whether they are affiliated with one specific company or are independent, insurance agents can only sell insurance. They can't sell investment products such as mutual funds, exchange-traded funds, and stocks or bonds unless they are properly licensed.

The problem is that since the retirement planning business depends a lot on insurance products, if you're only licensed to give financial advice, then legally you must refer any business your client needs in insurance to an insurance agent. Of course, many clients may only want or need investment products, which means there will always be a niche for advisors who stay purely advisors and get paid based on direct fees from the client.[6] This can create a dilemma for advisors who are only licensed to sell financial products because they can't sell insurance products even though those products may be helpful for their clients.[7]

When you limit your options by selecting a financial professional who can only provide you with specific products or lines of products, you're potentially shortchanging your retirement because you won't be able to avail yourself of the full universe of retirement planning products. As I've discussed in the first seven chapters of this book, retirement income planning is complex. Ensuring that you have access to all the products that you might need to execute the retirement income strategy that is best for you will help position you for success in your retirement.

SWITCHING GEARS

Now that you understand more about the role of financial advisors in retirement planning, we'll move into another important topic: taxes. As they say, it's not what you make, it is what you keep. And this couldn't be truer in retirement. In Chapter 8, you'll learn about how taxes can impact your retirement and strategies you can employ to minimize your taxes in retirement.

CHAPTER 8

TAXES IN RETIREMENT

TAXES ARE USUALLY NOT top of mind when it comes to retirement. When you're preparing for retirement, it's easy to believe the savings you've built over decades are exclusively yours to draw on for retirement income. However, in most situations, that isn't the case. If most of your savings has occurred within a traditional company-sponsored retirement plan such as a 401(k), or 403(b) or a traditional IRA, your savings will be subject to taxes in retirement.

This is just one reason why it is dangerous to ignore taxes. There are also many other reasons why taxes are significant in retirement. First, taxes are likely to be higher for the current generation of late-career adults approaching retirement and possibly even higher for the generation after them. Second, taxes on retirement distributions can impact your overall tax status, moving you into a higher tax bracket and triggering higher Medicare premiums and Social Security taxes. Third, because taxes are indexed to inflation, they will continue to increase throughout your retirement even if Congress doesn't actually increase rates. Fortunately, there are simple ways financial planners can help clients reduce and eliminate these penalties in retirement.

The federal budget deficit has been ballooning for over a generation, and when that happens so consistently one of the most readily
available ways for the government to address it is with higher taxes on
higher earners, who are the likeliest to have more assets invested for
retirement.[1]

Also, there's an ongoing commitment no matter which party is in
control of government to maintain the entitlement programs,
including Social Security, Medicare and Medicaid. These programs
are at some risk for insolvency in the future, which means that
Congress might decide to increase taxes to prop up their finances.[2][3]
Finally, since former President Trump and the GOP's Tax Cuts and
Jobs Act in 2017, taxes are the lowest they have been in living
memory.[4] It's likely that before too long, taxes will increase. Therefore, it is a good idea to count on higher taxes in retirement and plan
accordingly.

ADVANTAGES OF A BUCKETS APPROACH

The buckets approach can be a planning tool for retirement. When it
comes to planning for taxes, a three-bucket approach works well:

- The taxable bucket
- The tax-deferred bucket
- The tax-free bucket

Because saving for retirement in tax-deferred vehicles like traditional 401(k)s, 403(b)s and traditional IRAs is common and popular,
many people end up with most of their savings in these accounts.
That means during retirement, a significant amount of taxes will be
due when you remove funds to pay for expenses and meet required
minimum distribution rules. When you initially saved those funds,
you received a tax deduction, so when you take money out of those
accounts, the government will tax it.

Essentially, you've been treating these accounts like they're yours and yours alone, when in fact you have the Internal Revenue Service as a "business partner," essentially owning a portion of those accounts. Obviously, no one wants to have the IRS as a business partner, but since this system of tax-deferred retirement accounts was popular for so long, there are millions of retirees who are in the situation of owing taxes on most of their retirement savings.

How exactly does this system work? Let's review. During your working years, it is easy to save money in a company-sponsored 401(k) or 403(b) account. Many of these retirement plans include company-sponsored matches, which in 2022 averaged 3.5%.[5] That means if your salary was $75,000, for example, your company matched your contributions up to $2,625. Those matching dollars are essentially free money, which is great. Both you and the company got a tax deduction when you contributed those funds to your retirement account.

During your career, you and your company likely continued to contribute to your retirement account. If you ended up with an account value of $500,000 when you retired, you'd be required to begin paying taxes on your distributions when you took money out of the account upon retirement or at age 72. Age 72 is when required minimum distributions begin, which means that the IRS requires you to take a certain percentage of your retirement funds out whether you need the money or not. Then you must pay taxes on that distribution. How much you have to take out depends on calculations prescribed by the Internal Revenue Service based on your life expectancy.[6]

The IRS states that you must take your first RMD by December 31 of the year that you turn 72.[7] Fortunately, most IRA custodians–the companies that manage retirement accounts on your behalf–can take care of making the calculations and withdrawal the money automatically each year. Your tax preparer, if you have one, can help you figure out how much you owe. If you prepare your taxes yourself, the tax prep software will also do some calculations for you to make this process easier.

A RETIREMENT TAX CASE STUDY

If you work with a fiduciary financial advisor in the years before you retire and have to begin taking distributions, that advisor can help you plan how to potentially minimize your tax liabilities in retirement.

To illustrate how this might work, I'll invoke a fictional client in a hypothetical scenario. This isn't real investment or tax advice that translates directly to your personal situation. However, this scenario is an example constructed from my experience helping hundreds of clients with retirement financial strategies and with some lessons that are universal.

Our client, let's call him Alan, is age 66 and has a traditional IRA worth $500,000. Alan is in a tax bracket which gives him a 25% liability to the IRS, when you combine state and federal taxes. Alan doesn't plan to use this money for income in retirement at the moment; therefore, he's just letting it accumulate. However, retirement, health, family and other situations can change rapidly. Since Alan is smart, he's put that $500,000 aside, and may have to utilize it later.

Should he need that money in a pinch and wanted to withdraw the money over the next few years, at current tax rates, he wouldn't actually be able to take the entire $500,000, since he owes 25% of that to the government. With a 25% tax obligation on $500,000, it's easy to assume that liability will be $125,000. In a sense, this is the debt that his qualified retirement account carries.

Before proceeding to the difference between smart and not-so-smart retirement taxation strategies, I should be clear that this is a hypothetical situation and point out some assumptions about Alan. First, we are assuming his tax liability is 25%. Second, we will assume his IRA will grow at 5% annually in the future. Third, we will assume when Alan turns 72, he will have to start taking RMDs from that account, whether he needs the money for income or not, and those distributions will be taxable. Any money he doesn't use for income at this point can be reallocated to other financial vehicles, whose earnings will also be subject to taxes. So, we're also going to assume that he reallocates what he doesn't need from the IRA distributions to a taxable financial vehicle that, like the IRA, earns 5% annually. And finally, let's assume that Alan will live to age 90.

Although this is again a fictional scenario, assumptions like these are similar to the ones I construct when first planning for any client's retirement taxation strategy. Now with those out of the way, let's see how Alan and his advisor could work with those assumptions to plan a lighter tax burden.

Assuming Alan remains at a 25% tax liability and receives his RMDs once he reaches 72 per IRS rules, we find that if he does nothing to adjust his planning, he will be liable for $158,000 in taxes on the RMDs, actually a bit higher than if he were to withdraw and use the IRA funds for income when he's around 66-70 years old. But since he didn't need that money for income and transferred the RMDs, as we've said, to other financial vehicles, he has to pay an additional tax for those earnings as they come in, which over the course of his retirement adds up to $69,000. Finally, once Alan passes away, his heirs are required by the SECURE Act to liquidate his IRA and other remaining assets over 10 years. After running the numbers, it looks like $110,000 will be owed to the IRS by his heirs.

So, let's add it all up. Alan has $500,000 in his account today, and potentially over his lifetime that $500,000 will generate $338,000 in taxes. That's in the taxes he pays on the RMDs, taxes on the growth of the assets he reallocated to other investment vehicles he reallocates to them, and the taxes paid by his heirs on the death benefit. Whew! And here you were thinking that $125,000 out of $500,000 was too hefty a tax bill.

Now what if Alan had looked at this account with a retirement planner and taken steps to avoid this? His most reliable option, the one I would have told him to go with at any rate, would be to convert his traditional IRA to a Roth IRA. With a Roth conversion, Alan would go ahead and pay taxes on those funds in his account now, and then let them accumulate tax-free going forward. In other words, he would shift the money he had in the tax-deferred bucket to the taxable bucket. He's going to pay $125,000, a quarter of the account's value, to the IRS this year, and in the future, those Roth IRA funds are not taxable. He isn't required to take RMDs on this, so he doesn't have to switch them to other vehicles and get taxed again on earnings. His heirs won't have to pay taxes on the remaining value of his account after he passes away. The $125,000, paid up front, is Alan's total bill from the IRS on those funds rather than the $338,000 he and his heirs were looking at paying over the course of 30-35 years.

In this situation, converting his traditional IRA to a Roth IRA was a smart choice financially and at the right time because after age 72, when the RMDs start coming, it's too late. Alan can't convert it to a Roth IRA any more at this stage, so he's effectively locked into the less desirable strategy with taxes. That slow bleed will take almost 75% of what he'd put aside in the IRA in taxes over time rather than the 25% of the account he could have paid if he'd been smart and paid up front to the IRS with a Roth conversion.

WHY RETIREMENT TAX PLANNING IS IMPORTANT

The point of Alan's example is that the IRS is always a bad business partner when it comes to your retirement funds. However, you can make relatively simple moves in the near term to limit your liability.

In my practice, I build plans that do this through the variables of tax bracket, income, rate of return, income including Social Security, the age at which you get Medicare, whether you're married, single or divorced, to construct a tax strategy through steps such as Roth conversions that both limit your liability in retirement and don't increase your burden overly much in the now. You can be in control of your taxes, they don't have to be in control of you, and with the advice of a retirement-focused investment advisor like myself, they won't be.

CHAPTER 9

ESTATE PLANNING

UP TO THIS POINT, I've gone through a lot of material on how to secure your retirement future. Now, let's talk about what you leave behind. Essentially, an estate plan is a plan for distributing your assets after you pass away, and which has four primary purposes that I'll address in this chapter:

1. To protect your assets for your family and other beneficiaries.
2. To allow you to decide who inherits your assets.
3. To allow you to decide who will make necessary decisions on your behalf in case you pass away or are otherwise unable to make yourself.
4. To protect your assets, in certain cases of large and complicated estates, from excess taxation.

The goal of estate planning is to ensure that your documented estate plan follows your wishes and to minimize the taxes involved in your bequests. These documents must be prepared by a licensed attorney in your state.

Estate planning is useful for everyone, not just the wealthy, because it deals with your assets and property. In fact, the definition of an estate is all the property you own, not just your bank and investment accounts but cars, real estate, and other assets that are of value.[1]

The strict definition of estate planning is "the process of making plans for the management and transfer of your estate after your death, using a will, trust, insurance policies and/or other devices."[2] So as this indicates, I'll be going into the technical details of the documents and such that you need at the end of the chapter.

To go beyond the dictionaries, the why of estate planning is simple: It allows you to prepare in as much detail as necessary for what should happen to your assets while you're mentally sound and capable of doing so. Otherwise, these plans will be made by the probate judges and courts which don't know you or your wishes. In this chapter, I'll first define the estate planning process and its main actors, then outline the taxes that can apply to estates of certain sizes and types depending on where you live, and lastly identify the five basic documents you need when conducting an estate plan.

ESTATE PLANNING ISSUES

There are three major issues that play into estate planning: the legal process of probate, the executor of the estate, and the beneficiaries.

1. Probate is "the entire process of administering a dead person's estate... [which] involves organizing their money, assets and distributing them as inheritance, after paying any taxes and debts." Probate ends when all this has been accomplished. How long it takes depends on the size and complexity of the estate, but about a year is a good rule of thumb in most states.[3] As we get into in the wills and trusts section, some assets may avoid probate.
2. The executor is the person designated by the person leaving the estate who oversees the process of probate.

While usually we choose a close family member or friend to do this intimate work, in other cases, a legal or financial expert can be designated. The executor is responsible for making sure that the assets of the estate—after debts and taxes are paid—are distributed according to the deceased's wishes, and every executor holds a fiduciary duty to both the deceased and beneficiaries to act in their best financial interest.[4]

3. The beneficiaries are those designated to inherit the assets. It's important to note here that the beneficiaries may not just be the people in your will. When you set up a life insurance policy, IRA, brokerage, mutual fund or other account, you also are required to designate a beneficiary. That beneficiary will have an interest in your estate when you pass away unless you change the beneficiary. Since families and inheritance are messy affairs that can change a lot, it's incredibly important to make sure your account-listed beneficiaries match those of your estate, and to keep them up to date.[5]

TAXES

There are three kinds of taxes on the assets you leave behind to your heirs:

- Estate taxes are defined by the IRS as "the tax on your right to transfer property at your death." In cases of non-liquid assets like a house or car, the fair market value when you acquired these assets is used to determine the estate's gross value.[6]
- Estate tax applies to amounts only over the exemption limits. Federally, that limit as of 2022 was $12.06 million, meaning only amounts over that will be taxed at the rate of 40%. This means the majority of estates will

not be taxed federally, and for those that will be, there are some ways of avoiding these taxes including trusts that pare down the effective rate to well below that scary number.[7]

- A minority of states have specific estate taxes. As of 2022, these are: Connecticut, the District of Columbia, Hawaii, Illinois, Maine, Massachusetts, Maryland, New York, Oregon, Minnesota, Rhode Island, Vermont and Washington. While rates vary, there is a sliding scale based on size of the estate similar to income tax brackets, with the highest being 20% (Washington). Again, thorough estate planning can potentially lower these numbers in reality.[8]

- Inheritance taxes are state taxes occasionally assessed on assets inherited after the probate process. There isn't a federal inheritance tax. As of 2022, only six states—Iowa, Kentucky, Maryland, Nebraska, New Jersey and Pennsylvania—had an inheritance tax. Iowa's inheritance tax is set to lapse in 2025. An inheriting spouse of the deceased is exempt from these taxes, and rates vary based on the size of the assets and/or the inheritor's relationship to the deceased. Like with estate taxes, planning through trusts and in some cases gifts before you pass can potentially sidestep the rare but wily inheritance tax.[9]

- Gift taxes carried a federal limit of $16,000 per person, per year in 2022, which means that if you give that much or less to an individual, you won't have to pay tax on that gift.[10] The ultimate gift tax exclusion over a lifetime is $12.06 million per person. Like the estate tax, most people are unlikely to exceed this amount.

While inheritance taxes don't apply to most beneficiaries, your beneficiaries may owe taxes on property or assets they inherit from you at some point. For example, if your non-spouse beneficiaries such as your children inherit a house or stocks or bonds, those assets could be subject to capital gains taxes if and when they are sold. As of 2022, federal tax law provides for a step-up in basis upon death. That means that if you bought your house for $100,000 in 2000 and died in 2022 when it was worth $350,000, your heirs will only have to pay capital gains tax on the difference between the sales price and the $350,000.

If your non-spouse beneficiaries inherit your traditional IRA, they will have to take distributions within 10 years.[11] That's because the SECURE Act, which passed in 2019, eliminated the stretch IRA for traditional IRAs.[12] The stretch IRA allowed non-spouse beneficiaries to stretch an inherited IRA based on their lifespan. When you take distributions on a traditional IRA, taxes are due.[13]

At the time of the writing of this book, the IRS was drafting rules regarding the 10-year distribution.[14] If you inherit a Roth IRA, there are no taxes due, and no distributions are required.[15]

FIVE ABSOLUTELY ESSENTIAL ESTATE PLANNING DOCUMENTS

A will is one of the most essential estate planning documents. A will specifies who you want to inherit your assets and property after you die. It also includes your instructions for the matters that need dealt with following your death. Especially important is the designation of your executor and beneficiaries which we covered above. A will has to be signed and witnessed according to the laws of the state and after your death it is filed with that state's probate court by the executor.

If you die without a will, which is called "dying intestate," the management and distribution of your assets will come down to a probate court acting on state intestacy law—which is pretty much a worst-case scenario.[16] Unfortunately, a 2020 survey of estate planning lawyers reveals that 68 percent of Americans die without a will.[17]

If you have minor children when you're making out your will, it's important to designate guardians for these children. When designating a guardian, it is a good idea to identify a backup or contingent guardian in the case your first choice passes before you or is unable to serve as guardian.[18]

The healthcare power of attorney (POA) enables the person you designate to make the necessary healthcare decisions on your behalf in the event of your mental incapacity to make them yourself. As with designating future guardians of your children, it's important that this person is trusted and shares your views. You should designate a backup healthcare POA if the first designee has passed or is otherwise incapable of fulfilling the duty.[19]

The financial POA designates the person who will have legal authority to manage your property and finances for you in the event of incapacity: they would pay your bills, make deposits at your bank, manage real estate, pay your medical bills and use your finances to support your family as long as you are incapacitated. For those last two, it's important to make sure your healthcare agent and financial agent are individuals you trust and who could work together on your behalf.[20]

Finally, a trust is a legal arrangement that provides for the direct transfer—without probate—of assets from you after you die to your heirs. The documents governing a trust, much like a will, have to have set terms for management of these assets by a designated person, the trustee. A trustee, like an executor, is a fiduciary obligated to handle the trust in accordance with the documented terms and solely in the best interests of the beneficiary.

The kind of trust you need will depend on your own circumstances and those of your beneficiaries. There are also revocable trusts, which you as the grantor can edit or adjust the terms of as long as you're alive and capable, and irrevocable trusts, the terms of which are set in stone once signed. As I said before, the trust is a useful and many-faceted tool which enables a direct line of transmission for assets and property free from probate and in some cases estate or inheritance taxes which would otherwise be applicable.[21]

Once trusts are created, they must be funded with assets. In many cases that includes real estate such as your primary residence, your retirement and investment accounts, your bank accounts and any other assets of value. Trusts that don't have any assets are useless.

ESTATE PLANNING PROFESSIONALS

For help in preparing and executing estate planning documents, consult an estate planning attorney in your state. Because state laws vary, you need an attorney conversant with the rules in your state. That attorney can talk with you about your situation and help draw up the right documents. Once you review and approve them, you need to sign them.

Then you can either leave the original will with your estate planning attorney at their office or file it with your local county Register of Wills Office if that is a service they provide. Make sure to keep digital and/or paper copies in a safe place and make sure that your spouse, partner and/or close family members and friends know where these documents are stored. You may also want to forward a copy of your healthcare power of attorney to your family doctor.

If you're working with a financial advisor, it is a good idea to get your advisor involved in your estate planning. Your advisor can help you transfer assets into a trust if your estate planning attorney is creating one for you.

CHAPTER 10

RETIRE FOR L.I.F.E.™

THIS CONCLUDING CHAPTER aims to assemble the elements of retirement planning we have learned thus far into a coherent picture. It's my goal here to convince you that the Retire for L.I.F.E.™ method offers the best possible way to build your future in retirement, and that you can and should start putting these pieces together right now.

As we saw in the very first chapter, a lot of what's wrong today with what we call "retirement planning" is that it doesn't actually involve planning. Instead, advisors pitch products with little regard for your actual needs. There's a difference between products and plans in financial planning that doesn't only apply to retirement. A product can be any one of the financial instruments we use such as an annuity, stocks, mutual funds, exchange-traded funds and so on. But a plan intentionally arranges the most appropriate of these products around a specific objective, like retirement, in a way that reflects your goals while minimizing overall risk.

This is knowledge that Americans need that many don't possess. Four of five retirement-age people surveyed by the American College of Financial Planning failed a test on basic financial literacy. They also were uninformed about fundamental facts highly relevant to the financial planning process. This survey revealed that:[1]

- More than 50% underestimated how long a 65-year-old man was likely to live in retirement.
- 70% lacked a plan for funding long-term care needs.
- Less than 10% believed they will ever experience a long-term care need, while 70% of those over age 65 will actually experience a long-term care event in their lifetime.
- Less than one-third understood what a safe withdrawal rate was from their retirement savings.

Many people assume that if they don't have enough saved for retirement, they can continue to work. But that doesn't always happen. In fact, the Employee Benefit Research Institute reported in 2020 that half of the workers they surveyed–48%–said they retired before originally planned.[2]

As you learned earlier in this book, even if you have a financial advisor to help you with retirement–and many don't–that advisor isn't necessarily knowledgeable in the methods that will help you build a sustainable retirement. That's because many advisors, by inclination or more frequently because of their employment situation, consider it sufficient to provide their clients with certain products that fit their needs, but potentially, aren't the best fit for now or the future. In contrast, planning is a science that many advisors, including me, have cultivated. Retire for L.I.F.E.™, which is one of those systems, is a holistic and concrete method that enables you and others to position yourselves for a sustainable retirement.

RETIRE FOR L.I.F.E.™ FUNDAMENTALS

Let's take a few moments to reiterate the essential components of Retire for L.I.F.E.™:

First, recall that retirement savings goes in three stages:

- Accumulation
- Preservation
- Distribution

Accumulation occurs during the years when you are working. That's when you're saving–or accumulating savings–for retirement. Preservation occurs near the end of retirement, when you seek to preserve what you've saved for retirement. Distribution occurs in retirement, when you spend–or distribute the money you've saved–on your living expenses. To minimize sequence of return risk–the risk that the market will decline at the beginning of your retirement, the preservation phase is especially significant. You don't want to hit a bear market like the one that occurred during the financial crisis of 2007-09 at the beginning of your retirement, which could permanently impair the ability of your savings to support you for the rest of your retirement.[3]

In contrast to other methodologies, Retire for L.I.F.E.™ emphasizes preservation going into retirement. That way, your assets are less exposed to market volatility, mitigating sequence of returns risk. By changing the focus from maximizing returns to preserving your principal, there's less risk involved as you move towards retirement. That helps you sleep at night, understanding that your assets are less likely to suffer from a steep decline at the very point when you need them the most: the beginning of retirement.

FOUR BUCKETS OF RETIRE FOR L.I.F.E.™

Let's look at the four buckets of Retire for L.I.F.E.™, contained in the acronym.

L is for Liquid. In retirement, it's important to have a cushion of liquid assets in case you have a need that isn't covered by your ongoing income. Let's say your car unexpectedly breaks down and it doesn't make sense to fix it. Instead, you buy a new car. That's where your liquid savings comes in. You can use that money for an unanticipated big-ticket purchase without having to sell your investments. By providing for six months of liquid assets, Retire for L.I.F.E.™ ensures that you won't have to sell investments in a down market. This is important over the course of a 25 or 30-year retirement—or longer. Selling assets in a down market compromises your ability to grow your assets to cover other expenses that can occur in retirement, such as long-term care. Growing your assets for as long as possible helps to mitigate your risks and ensure that you won't be caught short later in retirement when you have a big need.

I is for Income. Retirement income functions as your paycheck during this part of your life. That's why the Retire for L.I.F.E.™ program focuses so much attention on sustainable income. This is composed of Social Security, a pension if you have one, and income from a guaranteed source such as a fixed income annuity. The goal is to piece together sufficient ongoing income from these sources to pay your ongoing bills, including utilities, gas, food, property taxes and other day-to-day living expenses. Once your income need is covered in this way, then the rest of your retirement savings can be invested for growth to mitigate the many risks of retirement. By relying on Social Security, a pension and income from a guaranteed source, you won't have to worry about the performance of the markets. This strategy also removes any reliance on instruments such as bonds or bond funds. These instruments are also subject to interest rate risk, especially during rising inflation environments like the one experienced in 2021 and 2022.[4]

F is for Future. With the exception of the COVID-19 pandemic, Americans are living longer. In fact, the most affluent Americans tend to live the longest. That means you and your spouse are likely to live into your mid-to-late 80s or 90s. Research reveals that towards the end of retirement, healthcare needs escalate, which requires a higher level of spending. A research report from RBC Wealth Management reveals that a 65-year-old couple retiring in

2021 faces $662,156 in lifetime healthcare costs.[5] While seniors age 65 to 74 spend an average of $13,000 on healthcare expenses, those over age 85 spend an average of $39,000 a year.[6] This is just one example of why the Retire for L.I.F.E.™ program emphasizes investing the rest of your savings–after securing your income needs–for growth.

Growing your savings will potentially allow you to keep up with the rising cost of healthcare while also mitigating other risks. Should you lose your spouse, you'll need more income to make up for losing one Social Security payment, paying higher tax rates and higher costs of living. The future in retirement is long, and there's no way to know exactly how that will play out. You may be a fortunate individual who doesn't need long-term care, or you may be among the 70% of those in retirement who do. When you rely on an evidence-based methodology such as Retire for L.I.F.E.™, you can sleep better at night knowing that your savings are working for you to provide both ongoing income and growth to pay increased expenses that may occur later in your golden years.

E is for Estate. This is not really part of retirement planning since it isn't your own future, but who among us would not want to leave our family at least something as a material legacy? The tools of retirement planning are therefore applicable. The Retire for L.I.F.E.™ program, in concert with an experienced estate planning attorney, can carefully determine how to shift your assets to minimize applicable federal and state taxes on estates and inheritances through such instruments as a Roth IRA conversion, which, by the way, is also highly applicable to your own tax future during retirement. The legal construction of trusts allows direct inheritance without probate in addition to providing tax benefits. Under estate planning we also find these specific documents: wills, medical and financial power of attorney, etc. These may be necessary for your own peace of mind as well as the peace of mind of your spouse, children and other heirs. Dealing with your passing will be difficult enough. Don't put your family through additional, unnecessary difficulty if you can prevent it.

YOUR PATH FORWARD

In 2021, Alliance found that seven out of 10 Americans expressed concern about retirement risks, including rising costs of living and future market downturns.[7] However, those surveyed who work with a financial professional are reluctant to discuss their concerns with their advisor.[8] Despite this reluctance, they would welcome conversations on topics such as longevity risk, market risk, investment risk, healthcare risk and more.[9]

What this tells me is that many people in this survey may need a different advisor. To me, not being able to discuss important retirement risks with a financial professional is a big red flag. Financial professionals and advisors need to be as pro-active as possible in bringing these topics up with their clients and helping them find the right solutions. As I've stressed throughout this book, those solutions begin with an assessment of your financial situation, a discussion of your goals and the creation of a retirement plan. At that point, discussion of the products best suited to execute that plan should be initiated—not before.

The goal of retirement income planning is to construct a framework for a sustainable retirement. Such a plan must meet your income needs while also creating a path to grow your assets to deal with potential retirement risks. There aren't any crystal balls. That means there is no way to know which retirement risks you will face and when they will happen. Perhaps an extended period of high inflation and market volatility is ahead of us. Or maybe not—perhaps you'll face some health issues during a long life. Whatever the risks that you do ultimately face, a sound retirement plan must be set up to deal with these issues.

That's the promise of the Retire for L.I.F.E.™ method. I can't promise you freedom from the many retirement risks that are out there. But I can say that with the right planning methodology and a sound plan, you'll be positioned for whatever risks do arise in the course of a sustainable, worry-free retirement.

Fortunately, using the Retire for L.I.F.E.™ method that I have outlined and in consultation with a qualified and independent retirement financial advisor, you can build a retirement income plan tailored to your individual situation. With Retire for L.I.F.E.™, you can position yourself successfully to balance the guaranteed income you'll need while mitigating the potential retirement risks. Retire for L.I.F.E.™ offers you the potential for a worry-free retirement.

NOTES

1. THE RETIRE FOR L.I.F.E.™ PROGRAM

1. "Financial Planning Founders Started a Movement – And Created a Profession," Investment News, Sept. 14, 2019, https://www.investmentnews.com/financial-planning-founders-started-a-movement-and-created-a-profession-81110
2. "2020 Census Will Help Policymakers Prepare for the Incoming Wave of Aging Baby Boomers, U.S. Census Bureau, Dec. 10, 2019, https://www.census.gov/library/stories/2019/12/by-2030-all-baby-boomers-will-be-age-65-or-older.html
3. "What is the History of the S&P 500?" Investopedia.com, April 5, 2021, https://www.investopedia.com/ask/answers/041015/what-history-sp-500.asp
4. https://www.macrotrends.net/2526/sp-500-historical-annual-returns
5. Nancy Mann Jackson, "How Long Do Downturns Last?" Acorns.com, March 10, 2020, https://www.acorns.com/money-basics/the-economy/how-long-do-downturns-last/
6. https://www.kiplinger.com/slideshow/investing/t052-s001-8-facts-you-need-to-know-about-bear-markets/index.html
7. Omar Aguilar, "Fundamentals of behavioral finance: Confirmation bias," Charles Schwab Asset Management, Aug. 28, 2020: https://www.schwabassetmanagement.com/content/confirmation-bias. Accessed Aug. 10, 2021.

2. RETIREMENT RISKS

1. "What is Sequence of Returns Risk?" RetireOne, https://retireone.com/sequence-of-returns-risk. Accessed Sept. 13, 2021.
2. "Longevity Risk and How it Affects Your Plan," The Human Interest Team, Jun. 8, 2020: https://humaninterest.com/learn/articles/longevity-risk-and-how-it-affects-your-plan. Accessed Sept. 13, 2021.
3. Kate Beattie, "Longevity: Don't Plan for an Average Retirement," Capital Group, Jul. 13, 2021: https://www.capitalgroup.com/advisor/insights/articles/ir-retirement-longevity.html. Accessed Sept. 13, 2021.
4. Interplex, "How Medical Technology Advances Extend Life Expectancy," Interplex, https://interplex.com/trends/how-medical-technology-advances-extend-life-expectancy/. Accessed Oct. 7, 2022.
5. Wade Pfau, "Changing Risks in Retirement, Part Two: Unknown Longevity," Forbes, Dec. 6, 2019: https://www.forbes.com/sites/wadepfau/2019/12/06/

changing-risks-in-retirement-part-two-unknown-longevity/?sh=5c8ce973652b. Accessed Sept. 13, 2021.

6. Mark Miller, "Retirement Healthcare Costs: Let's Get Real," Morningstar, Jul. 26, 2019: https://www.morningstar.com/articles/935728/retirement-healthcare-costs-lets-get-real. Accessed Sept. 13, 2021.

7. "What's not covered by Part A & Part B?" Medicare.gov., 2021, https://www.medicare.gov/what-medicare-covers/whats-not-covered-by-part-a-part-b

8. "Fidelity's Annual Retiree Health Care Cost Estimate Hists New High," BusinessWire, May 7, 2021: https://www.businesswire.com/news/home/20210507005403/en/Fidelity%E2%80%99s-20th-Annual-Retiree-Health-Care-Cost-Estimate-Hits-New-High-A-Couple-Retiring-Today-Will-Need-300000-to-Cover-Medical-Expenses-an-88-Increase-Since-2002. Accessed Sept. 13, 2021.

9. Anthony Bartlett, "Don't Let Healthcare Costs Make You Sick," TheStreet, Mar. 30, 2021: https://www.thestreet.com/retirement-daily/planning-living-retirement/dont-let-healthcare-costs-make-you-sick. Accessed Sept. 13, 2021.

10. Mark Hendricks, "Health Care is an Even Bigger Part of Retirement Planning," CNBC, Oct. 10, 2017: https://www.cnbc.com/2017/10/06/health-care-is-an-even-bigger-part-of-retirement-planning.html. Accessed Sept. 13, 2021.

11. National Council on Aging, "Get the Facts on Healthy Aging," Jan. 1, 2021: https://www.ncoa.org/article/get-the-facts-on-healthy-aging. Accessed Sept. 13, 2021.

12. Wenlaing Hou, Center for Retirement Research at Boston College, "How Well Do Retirees Assess the Risks They Face? July 2022, https://crr.bc.edu/wp-content/uploads/2022/06/IB_22-10.pdf. Accessed Oct. 7 2022

13. "Understanding Long-Term Care," LongTermCare.gov, Aug. 2, 2021, https://acl.gov/ltc/basic-needs

14. Rivan V. Stinson, "Plan Now for Long-Term Care," Kiplinger, Jul. 28, 2021: https://www.kiplinger.com/retirement/long-term-care/603187/plan-now-for-long-term-care. Accessed Sept. 13, 2021.

15. Rebecca Lake, "How Inflation Eats Away at Your Retirement Income," Investopedia, Dec. 1, 2020: https://www.investopedia.com/articles/retirement/052616/how-inflation-eats-away-your-retirement.asp. Accessed Sept. 13, 2021.

16. Steve Vernon, FSA, "Understanding Longevity: An Important Life Planning Step," Stanford Center on Longevity, 2017, https://longevity.stanford.edu/wp-content/uploads/2017/02/Understanding-Longevity-2.pdf. Accessed Oct. 7, 2022.

17. Charlotte Morabito, "Why health-care costs are rising in the U.S. more than anywhere else," CNBC.com, Feb. 28, 2022, https://www.cnbc.com/2022/02/28/why-health-care-costs-are-rising-in-the-us-more-than-anywhere-else-.html

18. Kelly LaVigne, "Managing Inflation Risk in Retirement," Kiplinger, Dec. 16, 2019: https://www.kiplinger.com/article/retirement/t037-c032-s014-managing-inflation-risk-in-retirement.html. Accessed Sept. 13, 2021.

19. "10 Things You Should Know About Bear Markets," Hartford Funds: https://www.hartfordfunds.com/practice-management/client-conversations/bear-markets.html. Accessed Sept. 13, 2021.

20. Carmen Reincke, "How to Navigate Volatile Markets During Retirement," CNBC, Sept. 24, 2020: https://www.cnbc.com/2020/09/24/-how-to-navigate-volatile-markets-during-retirement.html. Accessed Sept. 13, 2021.
21. "Navigating Retirement Savings between Volatile Markets," Blackrock: https://www.blackrock.com/us/individual/education/retirement-volatility-strategies. Accessed Sept. 13, 2021.
22. Reincke, "How to Navigate Volatile Markets During Retirement."

3. SEQUENCE OF RETURNS RISK

1. Wade Pfau, "Navigating One of the Greatest Risks of Retirement Planning," Retirement Researcher: https://retirementresearcher.com/navigating-one-greatest-risks-retirement-income-planning. Accessed Sept. 30, 2021.
2. Wade Pfau, "Navigating One of the Greatest Risks of Retirement Planning," Retirement Researcher: https://retirementresearcher.com/navigating-one-greatest-risks-retirement-income-planning. Accessed Sept. 30, 2021
3. Wade Pfau, "Navigating One of the Greatest Risks of Retirement Planning," Retirement Researcher: https://retirementresearcher.com/navigating-one-greatest-risks-retirement-income-planning. Accessed Sept. 30, 2021
4. Amy C. Arnott, "Sequence of Returns Risk: What It Means and How to Deal," Morningstar, Aug. 3, 2020: https://www.morningstar.com/articles/995102/sequence-of-returns-what-it-means-and-how-to-deal. Accessed Sept. 30, 2021.
5. "United States Stock Market Index (US30)," Trading Economics.com, https://tradingeconomics.com/united-states/stock-market

4. TWO TYPES OF INVESTMENTS

1. Your Retirement Reality, "Guaranteed vs. non-guaranteed income sources," https://www.yourretirementreality.com/guaranteed-vs-non-guaranteed-income-sources. Accessed Nov. 10, 2021.
2. "Deposit Insurance At A Glance," Federal Deposit Insurance Corporation, Oct. 15, 2021, https://www.fdic.gov/resources/deposit-insurance/brochures/deposits-at-a-glance/
3. "Types of investments available for Nationwide investment products," Nationwide, https://www.nationwide.com/lc/resources/investing-and-retirement/articles/investment-types. Accessed Nov. 10, 2021.
4. "Panic in the Parking Lot for Cash," The New York Times, Oct. 9, 2020, https://www.nytimes.com/2020/10/09/business/mutfund/money-market-funds-low-interest-rates.html
5. "What is a fixed index annuity?" Nationwide, https://www.nationwide.com/lc/resources/investing-and-retirement/articles/what-is-a-fixed-indexed-annuity. Accessed Nov. 10, 2021.
6. "U.S. Treasury Securities," FINRA, https://tradingeconomics.com/united-states/stock-market

7. "Search for Yield Sustains Buoyant Markets," Bank of International Settlements, Dec. 7, 2022, https://www.bis.org/publ/qtrpdf/r_qt2012a.htm

8. "Why did 30-year Mortgage Rates Go as High as 18.45 Percent in 1981?" Loanatik.com, https://www.loanatik.com/827-2/

9. "What's a REIT?" Nareit, https://www.reit.com/what-reit. Accessed Nov. 10, 2021.

10. U.S. Securities and Exchange Commission, Office of Investor Education and Advocacy, "Variable annuities: What you should know," https://www.sec.gov/investor/pubs/sec-guide-to-variable-annuities.pdf. Accessed Nov. 10, 2021.

11. Ken Nuss, "Retirees with a guaranteed income are happier, live longer," Kiplinger, Dec. 24, 2020: https://www.kiplinger.com/retirement/annuities/601986/retirees-with-a-guaranteed-income-are-happier-live-longer?aid=1065179&data=aWlkPTYxJnVpZD0xNjAzNjg3MDI=. Accessed Nov. 10, 2021.

5. ANNUITIES 101

1. Insurance Information Institute, "What are the different types of annuities?" https://www.iii.org/article/what-are-different-types-annuities. Accessed Dec. 28, 2021.

2. Claire Boyte-White, "The Main Types of Annuities Made Easy," Investopedia, May 30, 2021: https://www.investopedia.com/ask/answers/093015/what-are-main-kinds-annuities.asp. Accessed Dec. 28, 2021.

3. US Securities and Exchange Commission, "Annuities," https://www.investor.gov/introduction-investing/investing-basics/investment-products/insurance-products/annuities. Accessed Dec. 28, 2021.

4. Shawn Plummer, "Understanding the Different Values in Annuities," The Annuity Expert, https://www.annuityexpertadvice.com/annuity-101/annuity-values/

5. Shawn Plummer, "Understanding the Different Values in Annuities," The Annuity Expert, https://www.annuityexpertadvice.com/annuity-101/annuity-values/

6. Shawn Plummer, "Understanding the Different Values in Annuities," The Annuity Expert, https://www.annuityexpertadvice.com/annuity-101/annuity-values/

7. Stan Garrison Haithcock, "How Annuity Riders Work and Tips for Choosing One," The Balance, Nov. 30, 2020: https://www.thebalance.com/what-is-an-annuity-rider-146001. Accessed Dec. 28, 2021.

8. Ibid.

6. CLAIMING SOCIAL SECURITY

1. Social Security Administration, "Starting Your Retirement Benefits Early," https://www.ssa.gov/benefits/retirement/planner/agereduction.html, accessed Feb. 4, 2019.

2. Social Security Administration, "Program Explainer: Benefit Claiming Age," Nov. 2019: https://www.ssa.gov/policy/docs/program-explainers/benefit-claiming-age.pdf. Accessed Feb. 4, 2022.

3. "Social Security Solvency Could Lead to Lower Benefits for Millennials," GoBankingRates.com, Aug. 4, 2022, https://www.gobankingrates.com/retirement/social-security/social-security-solvency-lower-benefits-for-millennials/

4. Social Security Administration, "Starting Your Retirement Benefits Early," https://www.ssa.gov/benefits/retirement/planner/agereduction.html, accessed Feb. 4, 2019.

5. Melissa Horton, "How Do I Calculate My Social Security Break-Even Age?" Investopedia, Nov. 17, 2021, https://www.investopedia.com/ask/answers/020615/how-do-i-calculate-my-social-security-breakeven-age.asp. Accessed Feb. 4, 2022.

6. Ken Moraif, "How to Calculate the Breake-Even Age for Taking Social Security," Kiplinger, Aug. 30, 2021, https://www.kiplinger.com/article/retirement/t051-c032-s014-how-to-calculate-social-security-break-even-age.html. Accessed Feb. 4, 2022.

7. "Learn About Retirement Benefits," U.S. Social Security Administration, https://www.ssa.gov/benefits/retirement/learn.html#:~:text=Full%20retirement%20age%20is%20the,1960%2C%20until%20it%20reaches%2067

8. "Early or Late Retirement?" U.S. Social Security Administration, https://www.ssa.gov/oact/quickcalc/early_late.html

9. American Association for Retired Persons, "What is My Social Security Full Retirement Age?" Dec. 20, 2021, https://www.aarp.org/retirement/social-security/questions-answers/social-security-full-retirement-age. Accessed Feb. 4, 2021.

10. American Association for Retired Persons, "Can I Collect Social Security on My Spouse's Record?" Mar. 26, 2020, https://www.aarp.org/retirement/social-security/questions-answers/spouse-social-security. Accessed Feb. 4, 2021.

11. Social Security Administration Office of the Chief Actuary, "Benefits for Spouses," Sept. 25, 2013, https://www.ssa.gov/oact/quickcalc/spouse.html. Accessed Feb. 4, 2022.

12. Social Security Administration, "Receiving Benefits While Working," https://www.ssa.gov/benefits/retirement/planner/whileworking.html. Accessed Feb. 4, 2022.

13. Social Security Administration, "Receiving Benefits While Working," https://www.ssa.gov/benefits/retirement/planner/whileworking.html. Accessed Feb. 4, 2022.

14. Investopedia.com, "A Brief History of U.S. Bear Markets," Sept. 23, 2022, https://www.investopedia.com/a-history-of-bear-markets-4582652, accessed Oct. 7, 2022

15. Social Security Administration, "Income Taxes and Your Social Security Benefit," https://www.ssa.gov/benefits/retirement/planner/taxes.html. Accessed Feb. 4, 2022.

16. Beverly Bird, "What is Provisional Income?" The Balance, Feb. 3, 2022, https://www.thebalance.com/what-is-provisional-income-5200257. Accessed Feb. 4, 2022.

7. FINANCIAL ADVISORS

1. Casey B. Weade, "Is Your Financial Advisor Truly Independent?" Kiplinger, Aug. 1 2018: https://www.kiplinger.com/article/retirement/t023-c032-s014-is-your-financial-advisor-truly-independent.html. Accessed Feb. 16, 2022.
2. Weade, "Is Your Financial Advisor Truly Independent?"
3. Weade, "Is Your Financial Advisor Truly Independent?"
4. Securities and Exchange Commission, "Making Sense of Financial Professional Titles."
5. Jeremy L. Stanley, "The Difference Between a Financial Advisor and an Insurance Agent," CRNA Financial Planning, Mar. 29, 2018: https://www.crnafinancialplanning.com/blog/the-difference-between-a-financial-advisor-and-an-insurance-agent. Accessed Feb. 16, 2022.
6. Michael Kitces, "How Brokers and Agents Can Get Paid Directly For Delivering a Financial Plan," Kitces Blog, Mar. 29, 2018: https://www.kitces.com/blog/get-paid-for-financial-planning-broker-dealer-ria-hybrid-dual-registered.   Accessed Feb. 16, 2022.
7. Kate Stalter, "How Financial Advisors View Selling Insurance," *U.S. News & World Report*, Dec. 14, 2020: https://money.usnews.com/financial-advisors/articles/selling-insurance-a-hot-button-issue-for-financial-advisors. Accessed Feb. 16, 2022.

8. TAXES IN RETIREMENT

1. "U.S. National Debt Tops $30 Trillions as Borrowing Surged Amid Pandemic," The New York Times, Feb. 1, 2022, https://www.nytimes.com/2022/02/01/us/politics/national-debt-30-trillion.html
2. "Covid took one year off the financial life of the Social Security retirement fund," The Washington Post, Sept. 3, 2021, https://www.washingtonpost.com/business/2021/09/03/social-security-insolvency/
3. Social Security and Medicare may experience their own COVID-19 side effects, experts say," The Philadelphia Inquirer, Feb. 27, 2021, https://www.inquirer.com/health/coronavirus/how-will-covid-19-affect-social-security-medicare-disability-20210301.html
4. "How Did the Tax Cuts and Jobs Act Change Personal Taxes?" The Tax Policy Center, 2018, https://www.taxpolicycenter.org/briefing-book/how-did-tax-cuts-and-jobs-act-change-personal-taxes
5. "Average 401k Match: Everything Your Need to Know," Upcounsel.com, 2022, https://www.upcounsel.com/average-401k-match
6. "Retirement Plan and IRA Required Minimum Distributions FAQs, U.S. Internal Revenue Service, Feb. 22, 2022, https://www.irs.gov/retirement-plans/retirement-plans-faqs-regarding-required-minimum-distributions
7. "Retirement Plan and IRA Required Minimum Distributions FAQs, U.S. Internal Revenue Service, Feb. 22, 2022, https://www.irs.gov/retirement-plans/retirement-plans-faqs-regarding-required-minimum-distributions

9. ESTATE PLANNING

1. "Yes, You May Need an Estate Plan, Even if You Don't Have an Estate," Brighthouse Financial, Jan. 23, 2018: https://www.brighthousefinancial.com/education/estate-and-legacy-planning/yes-you-need-an-estate-plan. Accessed Mar. 22, 2022.

2. Patrick Hicks, "Estate Planning 101: What is Estate Planning?" Trust & Will: https://trustandwill.com/learn/what-is-estate-planning. Accessed Mar. 22, 2022.

3. "Probate Guide," Irwin Mitchell: https://www.irwinmitchell.com/personal/probate/probate-guide. Accessed Mar. 22, 2022.

4. "What Does an Executor Do?" FindLaw, Oct. 7, 2019: https://www.findlaw.com/estate/estate-administration/what-does-an-executor-do.html. Accessed Mar. 22, 2022.

5. "The Forgotten Step in Estate Planning: Beneficiary Designations," Rudman Winchell: https://www.rudmanwinchell.com/forgotten-step-estate-planning-beneficiary-designations. Accessed Mar. 22, 2022.

6. Internal Revenue Service, "Estate Tax": https://www.irs.gov/businesses/small-businesses-self-employed/estate-tax. Accessed Mar. 22, 2022.

7. Paul Reynolds, "Estate Taxes: Who Pays? And How Much?" Investopedia, Jan. 9, 2022: https://www.investopedia.com/articles/personal-finance/120715/estate-taxes-who-pays-what-and-how-much.asp. Accessed Mar. 22, 2022.

8. Ibid.

9. Tina Orem and Chris Davis, "Inheritance Tax: What It Is and How to Avoid It," NerdWallet, Dec. 22, 2021: https://www.nerdwallet.com/article/taxes/inheritance-tax. Accessed Mar. 22, 2022.

10. "2021-2022 Gift Tax Rates: I'm Generous but Do I Have to Pay This?" NerdWallet.com, March 2, 2022, https://www.nerdwallet.com/article/taxes/gift-tax-rate

11. "The Elimination of the Stretch IRA: 7 Strategies to Consider," Kiplinger, March 5, 2020, https://www.kiplinger.com/article/retirement/t064-c032-s014-the-elimination-of-the-stretch-ira.html

12. "The Elimination of the Stretch IRA: 7 Strategies to Consider," Kiplinger, March 5, 2020, https://www.kiplinger.com/article/retirement/t064-c032-s014-the-elimination-of-the-stretch-ira.html

13. "Retirement Topics – Beneficiary," IRS.gov, Sept. 27, 2021, https://www.irs.gov/retirement-plans/plan-participant-employee/retirement-topics-beneficiary

14. "IRS Minimum Distribution Proposals Baffles Financial Advisors, Bloomberg Law, Feb. 24, 2022, https://news.bloomberglaw.com/daily-labor-report/irs-minimum-distribution-proposal-baffles-financial-advisers

15. "Retirement Topics – Beneficiary," IRS.gov, Sept. 27, 2021, https://www.irs.gov/retirement-plans/plan-participant-employee/retirement-topics-beneficiary

16. Matthew Jarrell, "Will vs. Trust: What's the Difference?" Investopedia, Jan. 4, 2022: https://www.investopedia.com/articles/personal-finance/051315/will-vs-trust-difference-between-two.asp. Accessed Mar. 22, 2022.

17. "68% of Americans do not have a will," TheConversation.com, May 19, 2020, https://theconversation.com/68-of-americans-do-not-have-a-will-137686

18. Glenn Curtis, "6 Estate Planning Must-Haves," Investopedia, Feb. 27, 2022: https://www.investopedia.com/articles/pf/07/estate_plan_checklist.asp. Accessed Mar. 22, 2022.

19. Ibid.

20. "Estate Planning Checklist: 10 Documents You Need to Put Your Affairs in Order," Freewill.com: https://www.freewill.com/learn/estate-planning-101. Accessed Mar. 22, 2022.

21. Jarrell, "Will vs. Trust."

10. RETIRE FOR L.I.F.E.™

1. "4 in 5 Americans Lack Retirement Planning Knowledge: Survey," ThinkAdvisor.com, Sept. 17, 2020, https://www.thinkadvisor.com/2020/09/17/4-in-5-americans-lack-retirement-planning-knowledge-survey/

2. "How to Make Sure the Retirement Crisis Doesn't Happen to You," TheBalance.com, Oct. 22, 2021, https://www.thebalance.com/retirement-crisis-stats-causes-effect-3306215

3. "Stock Prices in the Financial Crisis," The Federal Reserve Bank of Atlanta, September 2009, https://www.atlantafed.org/cenfis/publications/notesfromthevault/0909

4. "Research from 44 countries shows levels of rising inflation across the world," World Economic Forum, June 23, 2022, https://www.weforum.org/agenda/2022/06/inflation-stats-usa-and-world/

5. "Taking control of healthcare in retirement," RBC Wealth Management, 2021, https://www.rbcwealthmanagement.com/_assets/documents/insights/taking-control-of-health-care-in-retirement.pdf

6. "Taking control of healthcare in retirement," RBC Wealth Management, 2021, https://www.rbcwealthmanagement.com/_assets/documents/insights/taking-control-of-health-care-in-retirement.pdf

7. "Conversation Conundrum – Despite Lingering Worry, Majority of Americans are Reluctant to Discuss Retirement Concerns," Allianz, June 22, 2022, https://www.allianzlife.com/about/newsroom/2021-press-releases/majority-of-americans-are-reluctant-to-discuss-retirement-concerns

8. "Conversation Conundrum – Despite Lingering Worry, Majority of Americans are Reluctant to Discuss Retirement Concerns," Allianz, June 22, 2022, https://www.allianzlife.com/about/newsroom/2021-press-releases/majority-of-americans-are-reluctant-to-discuss-retirement-concerns

9. "Conversation Conundrum – Despite Lingering Worry, Majority of Americans are Reluctant to Discuss Retirement Concerns," Allianz, June 22, 2022, https://www.allianzlife.com/about/newsroom/2021-press-releases/majority-of-americans-are-reluctant-to-discuss-retirement-concerns

or investment advice. Neither CreativeOne Wealth, LLC or BrightPath provide tax or legal advice. For answers to specific questions and before making any decisions, please consult a qualified attorney or tax advisor. These concepts were derived under current laws and regulations. Changes in the law or regulations may affect the information provided.

BrightPath can provide information, but not advice related to social security benefits. Clients should seek guidance from the Social Security Administration regarding their particular situation. BrightPath may be able to identify potential retirement income gaps and may introduce insurance products, such as an annuity, as a potential solution. Social Security benefit payout rates can and will change at the sole discretion of the Social Security Administration. For more information, please direct your clients to a local Social Security Administration office or visit www.ssa.gov.

No Investment strategy can guarantee a profit or protect against loss in a period of declining values. Any references to protection benefits or lifetime income generally refer to fixed insurance products, never securities or investment products. Insurance and annuity products are backed by the financial strength and claims-paying ability of the issuing insurance company. Annuities are insurance products backed by the claims-paying ability of the issuing company; they are not FDIC insured; are not obligations or deposits of, and are not guaranteed or underwritten by any bank, savings and loan or credit union or its affiliates; are unrelated to and not a condition of the provision or term of any banking service or activity. Annuities are long-term products of the insurance industry designed for retirement income. They contain some limitations, including possible withdrawal charges and a market value adjustment that could affect contract values. Product features vary by state and restrictions may apply, including possible withdrawal charges. Please contact your agent or the Company for more information. Guaranteed lifetime income available through annuitization or the purchase of an optional lifetime income rider, a benefit for which an annual premium is charged. All examples provided are hypothetical and provided for illustrative purposes only; it does not represent a real-life scenario and should not be construed as advice designed to meet the particular needs of an individual's situation.

Your C1W disclosure should be in the front of the book.

ABOUT THE AUTHOR

Matthew Schuller, President & Founder of BrightPath Wealth Management, has 17-plus years of experience in the financial industry.

He wants his clients to know how their money is working for them. He wants people to be informed about wealth management. The more they know, the better he feels he's done his job as their wealth manager. Matthew is a fiduciary, which he takes very seriously. You will hear him say that most people have a product not a plan. Working with Matthew, you'll see there is a big difference on what he considers a plan compared to others.

Matthew is driven to share his financial and retirement knowledge with the general public as a successful, published book author and contributor to *Kiplinger*. He also travels the country as a keynote speaker to enlighten audiences on retirement and financial topics.

He is a devoted husband and father of two little boys. During his free time, he enjoys family time and coaching basketball.

To learn more, please visit: www.brightpathwm.com

Made in the USA
Middletown, DE
11 July 2025

10224883R00056